THE NUWAVE OVEN® COOKBOOK

Legal Disclaimer

DO YOU WANT COOKBOOKS LIKE THIS FOR FREE?

Get hundreds of amazing popular recipes in a convenient cookbook each month absolutely free. No catch.

Yes! You read correctly. We are doing this to build loyal fans who enjoy our work and support us through reviews.

You are not obligated to do anything. But if you like our cookbooks, please consider leaving a review on Amazon for us!It only takes you a minute, but leaves a huge impact for us as it helps new readers discover us.

SIGN UP NOW
COOKINGWITHAFOODIE.COM

Contents

Introduction

1. New to The Nuwave Oven®

a. What is an infrared oven?

As the name might give away, an infrared oven heats up food using infrared radiation. This heat source provides a faster and easier approach to preparing food, as opposed to the standard convection or conduction style. Infrared ovens can not only cook food by pre-heating, but also by shrinking, drying, fusing, and even baking; leaving a variety of options in which it can be used. Commercially, infrared ovens have many important purposes in processing and manufacturing food, but smaller models are used mainly for home appliances.

The main difference between traditional ovens and infrared ovens is the way in which they maneuver the heat and warm up the food. Convection and conduction processes involve the heat going through the outer surface to reach the inner parts, eventually heating both the inside and the outside. Infrared, on the other hand, directly penetrates the outside texture and affects the inner parts. This essentially means that the inside gets most of the heat and is warmed up much faster compared to the traditional ways. Another advantage of infrared ovens is that they can double up as a toaster.

b. What is induction cooking?

Induction cooking is generated by a series of magnetic coils that are present inside the oven. The magnetic fields that are produced can warm steel and iron utensils, heating any food that is in them. This requires less energy in the long run, and because of this, induction cooking is considered eco-friendly compared to the traditional ovens. The magnetic fields only affect specific areas of the utensil, so other areas do not get heated up and remains cool to the touch.

There are several benefits of induction cooking, as explained below.

1. Energy conservation:

Induction cooking uses only 1300 watts of electricity to perform the necessary cooking. That is only about 10% of the energy used in any normal method of cooking, saving you a whopping 90%.

2. Safety:

Due to induction cooking not using an actual fire, it is a safe method of cooking for teenagers. An auto-shutdown feature is also present, and the food can be carried without the use of mittens, since only the bottom of the utensil is heated.

3. Fast cooking:

The Nuwave Oven® contains ten different degrees of temperature accessible to cook the food. There are additional six settings that can offer variety in your preparation methods.

4. Lightweight and portable:

The oven itself is very small and light, as it does not contain any heavy materials, making it portable.

5. Easy to clean:

The surface of the oven is smooth, so any spills will not stick to it easily. A quick wipe will ensure enough hygiene maintenance.

2. What can you make with The Nuwave Oven®?

From grilled meats and vegetables to pasta, grains, and rice, the Nuwave Oven® can work

with just about any food that can be heated in an oven. Since this is an infrared oven that uses induction cooking, traditional methods are not used, and it can work with both breakfast materials and desserts. This machine can heat bread, soups, and sauces, even stocks while also making excellent homemade fondues. The Nuwave Oven® is especially good with handling meat and warms up steaks and cutlets very nicely. With it, the meat's outer parts become crispy and chewy while the inside turns tender and juicy.

How to operate The Nuwave Oven®

The Nuwave Oven® is quite easy to use. The rack can be used in multiple ways (8 in 1 functionality). For frozen food, the rack will be 3 inches tall whereas for a turkey the rack can be flipped over so that it isn't too close to the power head.

The default temperature is 350 degrees Fahrenheit. However, you can change it and the range available is from 100 to 350 degrees

Fahrenheit. After setting your desired temperature, you will have to set a cook time. The cook time can be set in hours and minutes but not in seconds. From any temperature between 300 to 350 degrees Fahrenheit, the default cook time is set to 2 hours. On the other hand, for any temperature lower than 300 degrees Fahrenheit, the default cook time is 9 hours and 99 minutes. By hitting the pause or clear button once, you can stop the oven and check on your food and continue from there by just pressing the start button. Double pressing the pause button will clear out the cook time and will allow you to start fresh.

The Nuwave Oven® Hacks

a. How to make food crispy

Making crispy food is really easy with the Nuwave Oven®. For example, you can use a chicken it crispy from raw/frozen. You only need to take the pieces of the meat and put them on the cooktop surface. Sprinkle some seasoning and start cooking; about 12 minutes is fine at first. Flip it over and cook the other side the same way. The oven pulls away the fat from the chicken, which is collected at the bottom.

You can also fry the chicken by flipping over the grill. This allows the chicken to be cooked using the fats at the bottom, which adds nutrients to the meal. Frying will only take 5 minutes. Use a kitchen thermometer to check the temperature, which should be around 160 degrees. The juices indicate how well the chicken is done. Making crispy chicken might be difficult in other appliances, but not with the Nuwave Oven®.

b. Surprising things you didn't know you could make

Banana pumpkin bread, for example, is something that you can make with your Nuwave Oven®. Other examples are seasonal dishes and even exotic ones, which include feta cheese with lamb chops, turkey enchiladas, and even a gourmet pizza. For a quick meal, chicken casserole or creamy eggs are good options. For both dinner and lunch, you can easily make some bread and bacon. You can also easily make croutons, which are difficult to make otherwise.

You can dehydrate fruits. You can use those dehydrated fruits to make cakes in your Nuwave Oven®. Toasted nuts, baked potatoes, and other crunchy food can be made simply with the Nuwave Oven® as well as most standard meals, which include zucchini, muffins, granola, oats, tofu, broccoli, etc.

Breakfast
[Recipes]

Quick Apple Tartines with Ham and Brie

Bring a refreshing change to your palate with this killer combination of apples and ham, with melting Brie cheese making things even better. Tartines, being the French breakfast favorite can be very easy to make without all that hassle. Did we mention that two-step recipes actually exist? Yes, they do!

INGREDIENTS:

- 2 thinly sliced small apples
- 4-6 oz. Brie cheese cut into thin slices
- ¼ lbs. ham, thinly sliced
- 4-6 oz. Brie cheese
- 4 slices of French bread

Serves: 8
Total Cook Time: 15 to 18 minutes
Temperature Setting: 400 degrees

DIRECTIONS:

1. Place the bread slices on a cookie sheet and put them in the Nuwave Oven® to just brown the edges at 450 degrees for 5-8 minutes.

2. Taking them out, place slices of apples, ham and Brie cheese.

3. Put the tartines in the Nuwave for 8-10 minutes or until the cheese melts.

4. Removing from Nuwave, cut each slice of bread into four pieces.

5. Serve the 8 bite-sized tartines.

Parmesan-Marinara Baked Eggs

If you are looking for comfort food or an easy twist to add to your regular breakfast, this is just the recipe for you. This baked egg recipe has Parmesan cheese for the authentic French vibe and marinara sauce for that extra kick. Serve it with the toast at breakfast or dig in with a spoon at any time of the day.

INGREDIENTS:

- ✦ 1 cup marinara sauce
- ✦ ¼ cup Parmesan cheese
- ✦ ¼ cup whipping cream
- ✦ 8 eggs
- ✦ 1 tbsp. capers drained and divided
- ✦ salt and pepper to taste
- ✦ butter for greasing
- ✦ chopped chives, to garnish

Serves: 4
Total Cook Time: 10-15 minutes
Temperature Setting: 400 degrees

DIRECTIONS:

1. Greasing four ramekins with butter, cover their bases with ¼ cup marinara sauce each. Top them with capers.

2. Crack the eggs and pour them; 2 eggs per ramekin.

3. Add in 1 tbsp. whipping cream and 1 tbsp. Parmesan cheese into each.

4. Bake the eggs in the Nuwave Oven® till well cooked at 400 degrees, for around 10 to 15 minutes till eggs reach the desired doneness.

5. To garnish, top each ramekin with chives and serve.

Baked Lasagna Toast

While in the mood for some Italian treats, preparing full-fledged lasagna may seem a bit too grandiose. Thankfully, you can always prepare some cheat meals that take minimal. Discover authentic Italian flavors in this quick lasagna toast that is a delight to prepare.

INGREDIENTS:

+ 4 slices Italian bread
+ 1 part ricotta cheese
+ ¼ parts grated Pecorino Romano cheese
+ 4 oz. mozzarella cheese
+ 1 tbsp. olive oil
+ 1 clove garlic
+ 2 cloves garlic, minced
+ 1 zucchini
+ 4 plum tomatoes
+ 4 tbsp. basil leaves, thinly sliced
+ ½ tsp salt
+ ½ tsp ground black pepper

Serves: 4
Total Cook Time: 24-27 minutes
Temperature Setting: 450 degrees

DIRECTIONS:

1. Toast bread in the Nuwave Oven® at power level HI until golden for 5-10 minutes

2. Microwave zucchini, oil and garlic on high power in the Nuwave for 4 minutes. Add the tomatoes, ¼ tsp salt, and ¼ tsp pepper. Microwave for another 3 minutes.

3. Keep 2 tbsp. basil aside to garnish. Incorporate the basil leaves, ¼ tsp salt, ¼ tsp pepper, ricotta, and Romano cheeses.

4. Spread ¼th of the cheese mixture, mozzarella cheese, zucchini, and tomato mixture on each bread slice.

Toasted French Bruschetta

The signature crisp of this mighty bread staple is to die for, yet it is so easy to prepare! Bruschetta is also a great snack to enjoy when you invite your friends and family over. With the use of the Nuwave Oven®, the process becomes even easier and takes a shorter time.

INGREDIENTS:

- Extra virgin olive oil
- 4 basil leaves
- ¼ cup diced mozzarella cheese
- salt and pepper to taste
- 12 diced cherry tomatoes, diced
- ½ French Baguette cut into 12 pieces
- 1 garlic clove

Serves: 12
Total Cook Time: 2 minutes
Temperature Setting: 250 degrees

DIRECTIONS:

1. Toast the bread pieces in the oven at 250 degrees for 2 minutes.

2. Taking them out of the Nuwave, rub each slice with a clove of garlic and drizzle olive oil on top.

3. Incorporate the tomatoes, mozzarella cheese, and basil in a bowl along with salt-pepper seasoning and a dash of olive oil.

4. Put the tomato mixture over the bread or serve as a dip for the bruschetta.

Wee Muffin Pizzas

These little savory delights make great use of the traditional round English muffins. These are cute, hassle-free, fully customizable with toppings of your choice, and serve as great breakfast delicacies. With this open-ended recipe, you can make as many servings as you want!

INGREDIENTS:

+ pizza sauce of your choice,
  e.g. Bolognese, barbecue or Alfredo
+ mozzarella or parmesan cheese, shredded
+ English muffins
+ Toppings: pepperoni, bacon, vegetables, etc.

Serves: As many as you want
Total Cook Time: 8-10 minutes
Temperature Setting: 425 degrees

DIRECTIONS:

1. Using a long fork, poke each muffin through until they pop open. Spread sauce on each divided portion.

2. Sprinkle some shredded cheese on the muffins. Next, add the toppings of your choice.

3. Bake in the Nuwave Oven® at power level 425 degrees for 8-10 minutes, serve slightly cooled before you dig in!

Mini Muffin Pizza Delight

Any breakfast can be spiced up with the correct incorporation of Italian flavors! Using English muffins, pizza can easily become a bite-sized breakfast delight. This mini pizza delight is quick to prepare and is absolutely delicious in combination with Italian cheeses, pizza sauce of your choice, and eggs- also making it a hearty brunch option.

INGREDIENTS:

- ✦ 2 toasted and split English muffins
- ✦ ½ cup Italian cheese, many types blended in
- ✦ Oregano leaves, dried
- ✦ 1/3 cup pizza sauce
- ✦ 4 beaten eggs

Serves: 4
Total Cook Time: 10 minutes
Temperature Setting: 425 degrees

DIRECTIONS:

1. Gently pour the eggs in the Nuwave Oven® at 425 degrees for 5 minutes and pull the eggs forming soft curds. Keep repeating the process until liquid egg is no longer seen. Remove from heat.

2. Over the muffins, spread pizza sauce evenly. Also, top with eggs and cheese after placing on cookie sheet.

3. Bake in the Nuwave for 5 minutes till the cheese melts and then sprinkle with oregano after taking out.

Sausages with Maple Sauce and Figs

Using a maple sauce and figs with sausage might sound a little off-putting. However, the sweetness of the two balances out the meaty saltiness of sausages really well. Make some of your own to find out!

INGREDIENTS:

- 2 tbsp. Balsamic vinegar
- 2 packets roasted garlic sausages
- 2 tbsp. maple syrup
- 8 figs, ripe
- 2 tbsp. olive oil
- 1 ½ lb. Swiss chard
- ½ sweet onion, large
- salt and pepper to season

Serves: 4
Total Cook Time: 20-22 minutes
Temperature Setting: 450 degrees

DIRECTIONS:

1. Mix 1 tbsp. vinegar and maple syrup in a small bowl. Place the sausages and figs on a foil-lined Nuwave Oven® tray, brush with the mixture.

2. Roast for 8-10 minutes at 450 degrees till heated through and golden, brushing the remaining syrup during half time.

3. Microwave the onion on high power for 9 minutes in the Nuwave; add in oil, ¼ tsp salt, ¼ tsp pepper, and remaining vinegar and heat for about 3 minutes more.

4. Serve Swiss chard with the dish.

Quick and Easy Fritatta

It might sound pretty grandiose to prepare frittata at home, however, it isn't! Exotic flavors, rich texture, and wholesome goodness of vegetables make it a very healthy and filling breakfast. Try this foolproof, hassle-free recipe of this Greek classic that you can share with your family.

INGREDIENTS:

- ✦ 8 oz. Feta cheese, crumbled
- ✦ 3 tbsp. olive oil
- ✦ 2 tsp kosher salt
- ✦ 10 eggs
- ✦ 1 bag (5 oz.) baby spinach
- ✦ 4 scallions, thinly sliced
- ✦ 1-pint grape tomatoes halved

Serves: 4
Total Cook Time: 30-35 minutes
Temperature Setting: 350 degrees

DIRECTIONS:

1. Add olive oil to a casserole dish and bake for 5 minutes on 350 degrees.

2. Whisk the eggs with salt and pepper, adding in the tomatoes, spinach, scallions and Feta gradually. Stir gently.

3. Removing from Nuwave Oven®, pour beaten eggs into the dish. Put the dish back in the Nuwave.

4. Bake till knife comes out clean, for 25-30 minutes.

Cute Wonton Cups

Bite-sized breakfast dishes are always rewarding- you can eat without feeling guilty in small portions. These cute little wonton cups give you the oriental flavors you desire. Maybe you can take things a step further by making sweet instead of savory wonton cups!

INGREDIENTS:

✦ 6 wonton wrappers, cut into 3 inches squared

✦ 2 tbsp. melted butter

✦ any filling according to choice

Serves: 6
Total Cook Time: 8-10 minutes
Temperature Setting: 350 degrees

DIRECTIONS:

1. Press and fold each wonton wrapper into compartments of a 6-muffin pan.

2. Brush the edges of the wrappers carefully with butter. Bake these in the Nuwave Oven® at 350 degrees for 8-10 minutes till golden brown.

3. Put in your desired filling- either savory or sweet. Savory cup fillings can be sprinkled with cheese and Italian seasoning.

4. Sweet cups can be sprinkled with cinnamon sugar.

5. Fill warm cups with eggs or cool cups with chicken salad, pudding, or mousse.

Blueberry Muffins

Using cornbread to bake muffins makes many of us nervous; however, these healthy sweet bites are much adored and easy to bake. Blueberry muffins are a classic that everyone adores and relishes. The cute little muffins are a sure treat for the sweet tooth.

INGREDIENTS:

+ ½ cup buttermilk
+ 2 tbsp. sugar
+ 2 tbsp. apple sauce, unsweetened
+ 1 egg
+ 1/3 cup corn meal
+ 2/3 cup whole wheat flour
+ ½ cup blueberries
+ ½ tsp cinnamon
+ ¼ tsp salt
+ 2 tsp baking powder

Serves: 6
Total Cook Time: 20-25 minutes
Temperature Setting: 350 degrees

DIRECTIONS:

1. Grease a 6 cup muffin tray with butter.

2. Mix together cornmeal, flour, baking powder, salt, and cinnamon and set aside. In another bowl, whisk egg, buttermilk, applesauce, and sugar.

3. Add the wet ingredients to the dry ones all at once, mix till barely combined. Fold in the blueberries.

4. Dividing into the muffin cups, bake in the Nuwave Oven® at 350 degrees for 20-25 minutes or until a knife comes out clean. Serve with fresh cream.

Oven-Baked Eggs

If you are living by yourself or are just neck deep in work, this is just the recipe for you. This quick breakfast fix tastes great without the extra effort. Make as many as you like for your college roommates and friends!

INGREDIENTS:

+ 2 eggs
+ ½ tomato diced
+ 1 large spinach Leaf
+ 2 tsp milk
+ cheese, as required
+ butter, for greasing

Serves: 1
Total Cook Time: 15 minutes
Temperature Setting: 375 degrees

DIRECTIONS:

1. Grease a ramekin with butter.

2. Mix with two eggs, tomato, spinach and milk in the ramekin.

3. Sprinkle cheese on top of the mixture.

4. Bake in the Nuwave Oven® at 375 degrees for about 15 minutes. Rotate once.

Baked Pan Pizza

Everyone loves pizza from the takeaway, but did you know that you can make a homemade pizza which tastes just as great? This pizza recipe is straightforward and delivers excellent results. Try giving this recipe a shot the next time some friends come over for breakfast or brunch.

INGREDIENTS:

- ✦ 13.8 oz. pizza crust refrigerated and cut into half
- ✦ 2/3 cup Marinara sauce
- ✦ 2 cup mozzarella cheese,
- ✦ 18 slices of pepperoni
- ✦ 1 green pepper
- ✦ 2 large mushrooms, sliced

Serves: 8
Total Cook Time: 20-22 Minutes
Temperature Setting: 425 degree

DIRECTIONS:

1. Grease a pizza pan with 1 tbsp. oil.

2. Press half the dough into the pan. Bake in the Nuwave Oven® at 425 degrees for 8-9 minutes till light brown.

3. Put half of the Marinara sauce, 1 cup shredded cheese and half of the pepperoni, green peppers, and mushroom onto pizza crust.

4. Bake the crust in the Nuwave at HI power for about 11 to 13 minutes till cheese has melted and crust is brown.

5. Use the rest of the ingredients on a second pizza and bake.

Frittata with Zucchini, Mint, and Parmesan

Frittata tastes amazing in breakfast, bringing out the rustic charm of Italian cuisine. The flavors of this dish are what makes it amazing to share with the family. With garden fresh zucchini, refreshing mint, and the classic Parmesan cheese, this frittata recipe is sure to win hearts.

INGREDIENTS:

- ½ zucchini, julienne cut
- 2 tbsps. freshly grated Parmesan cheese
- 3 mint leaves, shredded
- 2 eggs
- 1 tbsp. olive oil
- salt and pepper to taste

Serves: 8
Total Cook Time: 25 minutes
Temperature Setting: 400 degrees

DIRECTIONS:

1. Beat the eggs, julienne cut zucchini and add all other ingredients. Place onto an oiled plate.

2. Bake for around 25 minutes in the Nuwave Oven® at 400 degrees and serve hot.

Fresh Harvest Granola

Granola is not 'just breakfast cereal', rather this healthy option contains different kinds of nuts and raisins to increase the taste of the traditional cereal. Moreover, granola is also great when you are really craving a quick snack. This harvest granola incorporates fresh produce, fruits, and nuts to make a healthy meal.

INGREDIENTS:

+ 3½ cup rolled oats
+ 1 cup assorted nuts 3 tbsp. mixed seeds
+ 1 tbsp. cinnamon, ground
+ ¼ cup grapeseed oil or other light oil
+ ¼ cup agave nectar or maple syrup
+ 1 cup shredded coconut
+ 1 cup dry fruits of choice
+ 1 tsp salt
+ 1 tsp vanilla extract

Serves: 6 cups
Total Cook Time: 8 minutes
Temperature Setting: 400 degrees

DIRECTIONS:

1. Line a baking sheet with parchment paper.

2. Combine and stir all the ingredients well in a large bowl. Spread evenly on baking sheet.

3. Bake for around 8 minutes in the Nuwave Oven® at 375 degrees.

4. Store in an airtight container after it cools.

Baked Oats with Apples

If you are looking for a healthy start to a chilly winter morning, this breakfast recipe is just what you are looking for. Oatmeal provides the creamy smooth texture while the apples provide a fruity touch. Go ahead and enjoy the goodness of oats and apples combined.

INGREDIENTS:

- ✦ 1/3 cup Greek yogurt, vanilla flavored
- ✦ 1/3 cup rolled oats
- ✦ ½ inch apple chunks, baked
- ✦ 1 tbsp. cinnamon, ground
- ✦ 1 tbsp. peanut butter
- ✦ Cinnamon, ground, for sprinkling

Serves: 1
Total Cook Time: 12 minutes
Temperature Setting: 400 degrees

DIRECTIONS:

1. Sprinkle the shredded apple generously with cinnamon and bake in the Nuwave Oven® for 12 minutes at 400 degrees.

2. Taking it out from the Nuwave, combine yogurt, oats, and peanut butter in a cereal bowl.

3. Serve while peanut butter is at melting consistency.

Banana Walnut Muffins

This recipe is for the little ones who love bananas, or everyone else with a sweet tooth. The walnut adds that extra crunch to these amazing muffins. This recipe will definitely be loved by the little minions running around in your house.

INGREDIENTS:

+ ½ cup oats
+ ½ cup whole wheat flour
+ 1 tsp baking powder
+ ½ cup golden raisins
+ 1/8 tsp allspice, ground
+ 1/8 tsp baking soda
+ 1 tsp salt
+ 1 banana, mashed
+ 1 egg
+ ¼ cup honey
+ 2 tbsp. canola oil
+ 1/3 cup walnuts, chopped
+ 1 tsp sugar

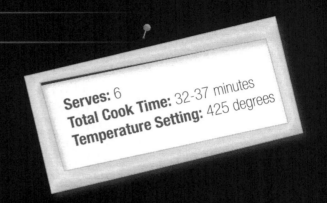

Serves: 6
Total Cook Time: 32-37 minutes
Temperature Setting: 425 degrees

DIRECTIONS:

1. Line 6 muffin cups with paper cuts and bake in the Nuwave Oven® for 12 minutes at 425 degrees.

2. Combine the oats, flour, baking soda, baking powder, allspice, cinnamon, and salt in a mixing bowl.

3. Mix mashed banana, egg, honey and oil in another bowl, stir gently. Add in dry ingredients till batter is moist.

4. Add raisins and nuts and stir in. Divide the mixture into 6 cups.

5. Bake for 20-25 minutes at HI power. Take out of the Nuwave when a knife comes out clean.

Oven Toasted Artichokes

Artichokes can look repulsive, but are really great to eat. Artichokes also have great food value and nutritious components. This toasted artichoke recipe will convert even those who loathe this vegetable.

INGREDIENTS:

+ 1 trimmed artichoke
+ 1 bay leaf
+ Kosher salt
+ olive oil
+ ½ tbsp. butter

Serves: 2
Total Cook Time: 15-20 minutes
Temperature Setting: 400 degrees

DIRECTIONS:

1. Washing the artichoke thoroughly, trim off the ends of the leaves and stem.

2. Put water up to 2 inches in a pot with a steam basket. Boil the water with a bay leaf.

3. Place artichoke on the basket and cover for 25-30 minutes till tender.

4. Slicing in half, scoop out the center of the artichoke using a spoon. Sprinkle each half with olive oil and salt and place in the Nuwave Oven®. Bake for 15-20 minutes at 400 degrees.

5. Serve with butter as a dipping sauce.

Grapefruit Glazed Beetroot

Looking for an interesting take on a popular vegetable? This is just the recipe for you. The rich red color of beetroot is a thing of wonder. Grapefruit glazed beets taste heavenly and rustic, tantalizing your taste buds.

INGREDIENTS:

- ✦ 3 lbs. beetroots
- ✦ 1 cup juice of 2 medium grapefruits
- ✦ 1 tbsp. rice vinegar
- ✦ 3 tbsp. maple syrup
- ✦ 1 tbsp. corn starch

Serves: 4
Total Cook Time: 50 minutes
Temperature Setting: 450 degrees

DIRECTIONS:

1. Trim the beet stems, dividing the beets to two groups. Drizzle with 2 tbsp. water and fold into an aluminum foil packet.

2. Bake the foil packets in the Nuwave Oven® at 450 degrees for 50 minutes till they can be pierced with a fork. Open the foil packets and let cool. Once cooled, slice thinly.

3. Add grapefruit juice, vinegar, and maple syrup in a bowl and stir. Measure the cornstarch into a pan and whisk in the syrup mixture.

4. Prepare a reduction by placing the sauce in a pan over medium heat, cook until it boils.

5. Serve with sauce drizzled over the beets.

Southwest Style Stuffed Peppers

Either rediscovering your Southwestern roots or simply in for a homely treat, this recipe is perfect. Do not be afraid, though, people of all ages can handle the heat of this recipe with ease. The stuffed peppers provide a tangy heat that is not too much, making it a delicious breakfast option.

INGREDIENTS:

+ 1 tbsp. oil
+ 1 onion, chopped
+ 1 garlic clove, minced
+ ½ pound turkey, ground
+ ½ cup black beans drained
+ ½ cup whole kernel corn
+ ½ cup salsa sauce, divided
+ ½ cup cooked rice
+ ½ tsp chili powder
+ ¼ tsp black pepper
+ 3 medium chili peppers halved and seeded
+ 1/3 cup Monterey Jack cheese, shredded
+ sour cream
+ coriander leaves, chopped

Serves: 4
Total Cook Time: 38-41 minutes
Temperature Setting: 350 degrees

DIRECTIONS:

1. Spray the baking pan with cooking spray. Heat oil in a large skillet, adding onion and garlic. Cook at 350 degrees for 2-3 minutes.

2. Add turkey in the skillet and cook for 6-8 minutes.

3. Add black beans, corn, salsa, rice, chili powder, salt, pepper and cumin in the mixture. Fill each pepper half with turkey, top each with remaining salsa. Bake in the Nuwave Oven® at 350 degrees for 20 minutes and sprinkle cheese to bake for another 10 minutes.

4. Serve with coriander and sour cream.

Baked Peach Cobbler

With an Nuwave Oven® at your disposal, making peach cobbler is child's play. Gone are the days of fiddling with peaches poached in water. Try out this easy recipe that makes a classic dessert easy to execute.

INGREDIENTS:

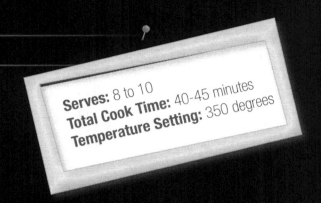

Serves: 8 to 10
Total Cook Time: 40-45 minutes
Temperature Setting: 350 degrees

- 8 peaches, peeled
- ½ cup light brown sugar
- ¼ cup corn starch
- 2 tbsp. lemon juice
- 1 tsp ginger grated
- 1 ¼ cup flour
- 1 tsp baking powder
- 1 tsp lemon zest
- ½ tsp salt
- 3 tbsp. milk

DIRECTIONS:

1. In a bowl, stir peaches, cornstarch, sugar, lemon juice and ginger till cornstarch dissolves.

2. Pour the mixture into a baking tray, greased with oil.

3. Stir flour, baking powder, lemon zest and salt in a bowl. Gradually stir butter and milk. Spoon this mixture over peaches.

4. Bake in the Nuwave Oven® at 350 degrees

5. for 40-45 minutes till the peaches are golden brown.

Lunch
(Recipes)

Glazed Salmon

Cleanse your palate with the natural goodness of fresh salmon. Salmon, as you know, is an oily fish and the benefits of having an oily fish dish in your food menu are of immense proportions. So include this delicious dish into your lunch and set yourself up for a great time with friends and family!

INGREDIENTS:

+ 1/3 cup sake
+ ¼ cup sugar
+ ¼ cup red or white miso
+ 1 tbsp. soy sauce
+ 2 tbsp. vegetable oil
+ 5 skinless salmon fillets

Serves: 4
Total Cook Time: 35 minutes
Temperature Setting: 350 degrees

DIRECTIONS:

1. Mix the miso, soy sauce, sugar, sake, and oil together. Coat the salmon filets with the mixture.

2. Transfer the mixture to a plastic bag and seal it. Let it marinade for 30 minutes.

3. Rub excess marinade off the fillets and place the pieces on the rack.

4. Broil in the Nuwave Oven® at 350 degrees until the tops of the fillets are charred and the salmon is warm at the center. Do this for 5 minutes and then get it out to serve hot.

Deliciously Roasted Asparagus

The classic, upscale combination of asparagus and olive oil calls for a luxurious treat to the senses. This dish has the benefits of being super healthy and super easy. So give yourself a break from the unhealthy food and munch on this healthy treat.

INGREDIENTS:

+ 1 bundle of asparagus
+ 4-5 tbsp. of natural olive oil`
+ salt
+ pepper

Serves: 4
Total Cook Time: 10 minutes
Temperature Setting: 425 degrees

DIRECTIONS:

1. Wash the bundle of asparagus thoroughly under running water.

2. Stack them up together and use kitchen scissors to cut one inch off of the thick top and bottom parts of the stems.

3. Lay out a baking sheet and arrange the asparagus stems over it, neatly placing them side by side.

4. Pat the asparagus dry with a thin cloth to remove all traces of water.

5. Pour some olive oil on top of the asparagus, while making sure that the oil covers all the stems evenly.

6. Sprinkle some salt and pepper over the asparagus.

7. Put the asparagus into the Nuwave Oven® at 425 degrees and roast them for about 10 minutes.

Chicken Tenders with Dijon Mustard and Honey Sauce

Chicken for lunch? Yes, please! Chicken tenders cooked with the moisture of the honey and the spice of the mustard- this is the perfect spicy dish for your lunch.

INGREDIENTS:

✦ 8 ounces of chicken tenders
✦ 1 tbsp. of olive oil
✦ ½ tsp. of herb mixture
✦ 2 tbsp. of Dijon mustard
✦ 1 tbsp. of honey
✦ salt and pepper

Serves: 2
Total Cook Time: 8-10 minutes
Temperature Setting: 450 degrees

DIRECTIONS:

1. Mix all the herbs, salt, and pepper together to use for seasoning.

2. Place the chicken flat over the rack and drizzle olive oil on the chicken skin as thoroughly as possible.

3. Bake in the Nuwave Oven® at 450 degrees until cooked through. This will take approximately 8-10 minutes.

4. Pour the honey and mustard into a bowl, stir together, and keep it aside.

5. Now get the chicken tenders out of the Nuwave, and serve them hot with the mustard and honey sauce.

Chicken Quesadillas (Tex-Mex Style)

Bring in a Mexican twist to the good old chicken recipe. If you are in the mood for something that will make you feel full, then opt for this during lunch time. It is the perfect spicy dish for you if you like the 'Tex-Mex' style.

INGREDIENTS:

- ✦ 2 big green onions
- ✦ 2 cups of chicken meat (shredded)
- ✦ 1 ½ cups Monterey Jack cheese
- ✦ 4 burrito-sized flour tortillas
- ✦ ¾ of a cup of salsa Verde
- ✦ ½ cups of fat-reduced sour cream
- ✦ ¼ cups of cilantro leaves
- ✦ pickled jalapeno chili

Serves: 4
Total Cook Time: 6-8 minutes
Temperature Setting: 425 degrees

DIRECTIONS:

1. Slice the green onions very thinly, leaving out 2 tbsp. of the green parts at the top to be used as garnish later.

2. Take one tortilla and divide it into a half. Put equal portions of chicken, jalapeno, cheese, cilantro, and the remaining parts of the green on one side of the folded tortilla, and then put the other half over.

3. Toast the tortillas on a foil-covered Nuwave Oven® at 425 degrees for 6-8 minutes or until the tortillas turn golden brown and the cheese becomes gooey.

4. Take salsa and sour cream into a small bowl and mix together to make a paste.

5. Cut each of the quesadillas in half and serve with the sour cream and salsa sauce, with the sprinkled green onions on top.

Chicken Quesadillas

All the goodness of chicken in one formula. This Mexican dish has the perfect balance of crunchiness and the freshness of the leaves as well as the gooey cheesiness.

INGREDIENTS:

- 4 flour tortillas, 8 inches
- 6 oz. Southwestern chicken strips
- 10 oz. diced tomatoes and green chilies, well-drained
- 4 oz. shredded Mexican blended cheese
- sliced ripe olives, shredded lettuce, and chopped tomatoes (optional)

Serves: 4
Total Cook Time: 10 minutes
Temperature Setting: 425 degrees

DIRECTIONS:

1. Take cooking spray and spray on one side of 2 tortillas to completely coat it.

2. Place the sprayed side of the tortillas directly on the rack.

3. Mix chicken strips, cheese, and sliced tomatoes.

4. Place the mixture on the tortillas and then cover the mixture with another tortilla and then spray the cooking spray again on top of both of the tortillas.

5. Bake in the Nuwave Oven® at 425 degrees for 10 minutes until the tortillas turn golden brown.

6. Get them out and cut them into wedges.

7. Garnish with the sliced olives, lettuce, and the tomatoes. This is optional.

Roasted Broccoli and Crispy Prosciutto

When veg meets non-veg. Accessorize your healthy broccoli pieces with strips of bacon and fat to get the best of both worlds.

INGREDIENTS:

+ 2 large cups of cut broccoli pieces
+ 2 tbsp. of any fat of your choice
+ 2 tbsp. of balsamic vinegar
+ 2-3 slices of sliced prosciutto
+ salt and pepper to taste

Serves: 4
Total Cook Time: 30 minutes
Temperature Setting: 400 degrees

DIRECTIONS:

1. Evenly place broccoli in a single layer on the foil-lined baking tray.

2. Now drizzle the fat on top of the broccoli and add salt and pepper to it. Toss and turn to distribute the fat all through the broccoli pieces.

3. When the broccoli is done, drizzle the balsamic vinegar on top.

4. Now put the baking tray onto the liner pan of the Nuwave Oven® and leave the broccoli to roast for 30 minutes at 400 degrees. Once done, set it aside.

5. Take the prosciutto and then again lay them out in a single layer on the baking tray.

6. Put the prosciutto into the Nuwave and roast for 10 minutes. Flip the sides when you are halfway through the cooking and then finally remove them and cool them down on a cooling rack so that they become crunchy and crispy.

7. Now add the crispy prosciutto pieces on top of the broccoli and serve on a nice plate.

Pesto Burgers

Italians love burgers too, and this recipe proves just that. Discover this healthier way to make burgers and enjoy it with a zero compromise on taste. The tomatoes, cheese, and the basil leaves create a combo that is absolutely hard to resist!

INGREDIENTS:

+ 4 Portobello mushrooms
+ 4 hamburger buns
+ ¼ cups of sun dried tomato
+ 1 whole ripe tomato
+ 1 log of goat cheese
+ 7 large and fresh basil leaves

Serves: 4
Total Cook Time: 23 minutes
Temperature Setting: 425 degrees

DIRECTIONS:

1. Place the mushrooms on the foil-lined tray and put them onto the liner pan of the Nuwave Oven® for 15 minutes at 425 degrees.

2. Now get the tray out, flip the mushrooms, spread 1tbsp. of pesto over them, and bake again for 8 minutes at HI.

3. Get the mushrooms out and toast the buns on the sides and get them out.

4. Place two slices of tomato, one mushroom, two basil leaves, and two pieces of goat cheese on top of the bun, and then finish it off with another bun on the top.

Zucchini and Squash Pizza

Vegetarians, the next time they tell you that there can never be a pizza without meat, prove them wrong with this recipe. And if you are one to think that vegetarians don't have fun with their food, then you MUST try this and prove yourself wrong.

INGREDIENTS:

+ 1 batch of crusts
+ 1 thinly sliced zucchini
+ 1 thinly sliced yellow squash
+ ½ cup of Parmesan cheese
+ 4-5 tbsp. of chopped herbs
+ olive oil
+ salt and pepper

Serves: 4
Total Cook Time: 12 minutes
Temperature Setting: 350 degrees

DIRECTIONS:

1. Divide the pizza dough into 7 small balls, roll out each ball, and lightly dust flour on the surface.

2. Add Parmesan cheese and fresh herbs to each of the small dough balls.

3. Add the zucchini and squash on the top of the cheese and herbs and lightly brush olive oil over them. Add salt and pepper to taste.

4. Put them into the Nuwave Oven® and bake for 12 minutes at 350 degrees or until the crust gets cooked.

5. Remove the tray from the Nuwave and let it cool before serving.

Paleo Pizza for the Family

Perhaps the quickest and tastiest pizza ever. Paleo Pizza comes with a package deal for the whole family. Make a large one for all of you and get appreciated for your amazing cooking skills after just 25 minutes of work in the kitchen.

INGREDIENTS:

✦ ½ cup almond flour
✦ 1 tsp. ground flaxseed meal
✦ 1 tbsp. egg whites
✦ ½ tsp. garlic powder
✦ salt and pepper
✦ ½ tsp. olive oil

Serves: 4
Total Cook Time: 15 minutes
Temperature Setting: 375 degrees

DIRECTIONS:

1. Combine all the ingredients together in a large bowl.

2. Roll the batter into small balls.

3. With a brush, lightly coat the ball with non-stick spray and then flatten the batter on a thin plastic into a round circle.

4. Put any of your favorite toppings over the crust and then put it in the Nuwave Oven® for 15 minutes at 375 until the crust is thin and crispy.

5. Get the tray out and use a spatula to remove the pizza from the tray and serve it as a snack to the family.

Yummy Squash with Kale

Clean eating only gets better when you have baked squash on the menu, and when you have kale added to it, the health benefits go up tenfold while adding flavor and deliciousness to the whole dish overall.

INGREDIENTS:

✦ 1 delicate squash
✦ 1 bunch of any green leaves
✦ 1 clove of garlic
✦ 2 tbsp. of olive oil
✦ salt and pepper to taste

Servings: 2
Total Cook Time: 21 minutes
Temperature Setting: 425 degrees

DIRECTIONS:

1. Wash the squash and slice off the ends and cut it vertically.

2. Put 1 tbsp. olive oil into the squash and mix it up.

3. Lay out a baking sheet on the tray, put the squash on top, and bake in the Nuwave Oven® for 20 minutes at 425 degrees.

4. Rinse the leafy greens while the squash is roasting and then chop the leaves up. Now chop the garlic clove into the greens.

5. Heat 1 tbsp. of olive oil on the stove and then add it to the bowl of leaves with a pinch of salt added to it. Sauté it until it turns a dark green color. Cook for another minute and add 2 tbsp. of water. Stir and remove from heat.

6. After getting them out, serve the garlic infused leaves with the squash pieces on top.

Salmon Sandwich— The Spicy Hot Version

Who doesn't like sandwiches? They are delicious, neat, and easy to deal with. And you can also experiment with the different flavors that you combine to make a sandwich to give birth to a culinary masterpiece. Try it with the healthy fish-Salmon, this time. Salmon sandwiches are a delight to make and eat!

INGREDIENTS:

- 1 piece of flatbread
- 1 salmon filet
- 1 tbsp. chopped green onion
- ½ tsp. dried thyme
- ¼ tsp. dried sumac
- ½ tsp. sesame seeds
- ¼ peeled and diced cucumber
- 1 tbsp. yogurt
- 1 zucchini cut into half
- 1 tbsp. pine nuts
- extra virgin olive oil
- 1 tbsp. fresh mint (optional)
- salt and pepper

Serves: 2
Total Cook Time: 6 minutes
Temperature Setting: 375 degrees

DIRECTIONS:

1. Cut the salmon fish on a slanted angle into thick pieces, place in the center of the flatbread, and add salt to it.

2. Sprinkle green onion, thyme, sesame seeds, and sumac over the salmon pieces.

3. Put the bread into the Nuwave Oven® and broil at 375 degrees. Keep it inside for 3 minutes until the salmon looks satisfyingly cooked (pink) and then take them out.

4. Now take a cucumber and yogurt in a bowl and combine them together.

5. After the bread is done, lay it out on a plate and then apply the mixture of yogurt and cucumber on the salmon and sprinkle mint on top.

6. Fold the ends of the flat bread into the center and press them together so that they lie flat.

7. Mix all the ingredients in a bowl and pour the mix onto the tray. Place the tray into the Nuwave and broil for another 3 minutes at HI.

Mouthwatering Pita Melts

Make this mouth-watering dish in just less than 10 minutes. Make these cheesy, delicious pita melts with sliced olives and onions and indulge in the goodness of the yummy pitas.

INGREDIENTS:

- ✦ 2 wheat pitas
- ✦ 1 cup of mozzarella cheese
- ✦ 1 tsp. extra-virgin olive oil
- ✦ ¼ red sliced onion
- ✦ ¼ cup of pitted Kalamata olives
- ✦ 2 tbsp. of chopped basil and parsley

Serves: 4
Total Cook Time: 2 minutes
Temperature Setting: 425 degrees

DIRECTIONS:

1. Brush each side of the pitas with olive oil.

2. Warm the oiled pitas in the Nuwave Oven® for a minute at 425 degrees.

3. Remove them after warming and add the cheese on top. Add the sliced onion and the olives. Put them in the Nuwave again.

4. Bake until the pitas look done and the cheese melts for another minute or so.

5. Spread the herbs over the pitas and cut and serve in the form of wedges.

Chicken Sandwich

Five minute meals are not a thing of fairy tales! This chicken sandwich recipe is perfect for picnics, during office hours, or for lunch when you need a quick meal to get your energy back up. It's simple, delicious, and very easy to make.

INGREDIENTS:

- ✦ 2 chicken breasts (use leftovers or pre-cooked chicken for this)
- ✦ 1 ripe tomato sliced
- ✦ ¼ cup of olive oil
- ✦ 4 oz. sliced mozzarella cheese
- ✦ sliced whole grain bread
- ✦ minced garlic (optional)
- ✦ 1/3 cup of basil leaves
- ✦ salt and pepper to taste

Serves: 2
Total Cook Time: 2 minutes
Temperature Setting: 350 degrees

DIRECTIONS:

1. On top of the two slices of the whole grain bread, put two slices of tomatoes and cheese. Then put them in the Nuwave Oven® and microwave for 2 minutes.

2. You can add the garlic over the molten cheese if you want.

3. Sprinkle the chopped herbs on the chicken and put the chicken over the cheese.

4. Drizzle with olive oil and season with salt and pepper.

5. Put another bread on top and serve.

Baked Coconut Shrimp, Infused with Chutney

Well, coconut, shrimp, AND chutney in one dish. Where can you go wrong, really? If you are one who likes to experiment with different cuisines, then this Malaysian dish is highly recommended for you. This exotic dish of the beaches takes your taste buds to an island far away, so be ready to treat your taste buds to the deliciousness of it.

INGREDIENTS:

Serves: 8 to 10
Total Cook Time: 10 minutes
Temperature Setting: 400 degrees

- 2 tbsp. green onions sliced
- 1 cup chutney
- ½ tsp. ground curry
- ½ tsp. flour
- 1 cup breadcrumbs
- ½ tsp. red pepper crushed
- Cilantro
- 1 egg white
- 1 pound jumbo shrimps
- 1 tsp. salt
- ¾ cup sweetened coconut

DIRECTIONS:

1. Get the chutney, curry, and red pepper in a bowl and stir until completely blended. Set this aside.

2. Spray non-stick cooking spray on a pan and set this aside.

3. Take a plastic bag and combine the salt and flour here. Add the breadcrumbs and the coconut to the bag, shake and move it aside.

4. Take the egg whites in a medium-Five-minute sized bowl and stir until they form a foamy texture.

5. Dip one shrimp at a time into the egg white.

6. Now place shrimp in the breadcrumbs and coat it completely. Arrange the shrimp in a tin-foiled baking pan and put it in the Nuwave Oven®.

7. Bake in for 10 minutes at 400 degrees until the crumbs become golden brown. Garnish with cilantro and serve with the chutney.

Delicious Crab Cakes with Creamy Sauce

Seafood goodness with a delicious creamy sauce- we all love crabs and we all love creamy sauce, so why wait any longer! Cook up this delicious meal in just 30 minutes and give yourself a treat!

INGREDIENTS:

Serves: 8
Total Cook Time: 10 minutes
Temperature Setting: 350 degrees

- ✦ 1 egg
- ✦ 3 tbsp. mayonnaise
- ✦ 1 tbsp. all-purpose flour
- ✦ 1 tbsp. brown mustard
- ✦ 1 tsp. seafood seasoning
- ✦ ½ tsp. salt
- ✦ 1 pound lump crabmeat
- ✦ ¼ cup chopped up parsley
- ✦ 1 minced shallot
- ✦ creamy herb sauce
- ✦ 1 minced garlic clove

DIRECTIONS:

1. Take the mayonnaise, egg, flour, seafood seasoning, mustard, pepper, and salt and blend together in a bowl.

2. After the mix is complete, add the shallots, parsley, crabmeat, and garlic into the mix.

3. Place mixture into a broiler pan and press down on it lightly so that it lies flat. Repeat this with the rest as well.

4. In the Nuwave Oven® broil the crab cakes for 10 minutes at 350 degrees.

5. Serve with the creamy sauce on the sides.

Mac and Cheese with Smoked Gouda

Take the everyday Mac and cheese and take it to the next level by incorporating the goodness of smoked Gouda into the recipe.

INGREDIENTS:

- 6 slices of cooked and chopped bacon
- 1 French baguette
- 2 tbsp. melted butter
- ¼ cup chopped parsley
- ¼ cup of flour
- 1/3 cup of butter
- 1 package of elbow pasta
- 1 packet of cheddar cheese
- 1 package smoked and shredded Gouda cheese
- 2.5 tsp Creole seasoning

Serves: 10 to 12
Total Cook Time: 26 to 28 minutes
Temperature Setting: 400 degrees

DIRECTIONS:

1. Drop the bread, parsley, and bacon into a food processor and get them finely chopped. Add melted butter and then blend again until the crumbs start to form, set aside.

2. Cook the pasta, drain, and rinse it out with cold water.

3. Melt the butter in the Nuwave Oven® at 400 degrees for a minute and then add flour to it gradually. Add milk and put it back in the Nuwave for 6-8 minutes. Remove from the heat as the mixture starts turning heavy.

4. Now add the cheese and the remaining bacon. Add seasoning to it and keep heating until the cheese melts away. Add the breadcrumbs into the mixture.

5. Pour the whole mixture into a baking dish evenly and spray it with non-stick oil spray.

6. Bake in the Nuwave again for 20 minutes at power level HI and then get it out to serve hot.

Eggplant Parmesan (Oven-baked)

This cheesy eggplant recipe is sure to win hearts at the lunch table and make praises instantly come your way. And if you like to make it cheesy, you are allowed to put in as much cheese as you want and eat to your heart's content.

INGREDIENTS:

- ✦ 1 eggplants cut into half
- ✦ 1.5 tsp. salt
- ✦ 1 cup of marinara sauce
- ✦ 1 package of sliced mozzarella cheese
- ✦ 1 package of freshly chopped basil leaves
- ✦ ¼ cup of parmesan cheese grated

Serves: 5
Total Cook Time: 60 minutes
Temperature Setting: 375 degrees

DIRECTIONS:

1. Sprinkle salt on eggplant and set aside to drain for an hour.

2. Spray the baking pan and five ramekins with nonstick cooking spray.

3. Rinse the eggplant with water to remove all the salt and drain each slice off all the water.

4. Put the eggplants in a single layer.

5. Bake it in the Nuwave Oven® for 30 minutes at 375 degrees and then place the slice on a cooking rack.

6. Layer 1 slice of eggplant on each of the ramekins. Add sauce, basil leaf, mozzarella, and sprinkle Parmesan cheese on top.

7. Bake in again for 30 minutes at HI until the cheese is completely melted. Serve hot.

Tilapia crusted with Parmesan Cheese

Cheese with fish. Sounds weird? It might, but like many things in life, this will come to you as a surprise- but a pleasant one, so it's all good to be tried out. This uncanny dish is, in fact, all set to become part of your family lunch hits.

INGREDIENTS:

+ 2 tilapia filets
+ ¼ cup bread crumbs
+ 3 tbsps. Parmesan cheese grated
+ ¼ tsp. black pepper
+ ½ tsp. seasoning
+ 1 tbsp. mayonnaise

Serves: 2
Total Cook Time: 15 minutes
Temperature Setting: 425 degrees

DIRECTIONS:

1. Spray the pan with nonstick cooking spray and then leave aside.

2. Add the breadcrumbs, cheese, seasoning, and pepper in a re-sealable plastic bag and shake it well.

3. Coat the fish fillets with mayonnaise on both the sides and then add the fish in the bag.

4. Press the crumbs so that they cover the fish completely and then place the ingredients of the bag onto the baking pan.

5. Bake in the Nuwave Oven® for 15 minutes at 425 degrees, then serve out on a flat plate.

Bake Sweet Potatoes the Savory Way!

This simple, elegant and sweet potato is full of textures and flavors that will blow your mind. This recipe is the perfect mixture of sweet and savory that will tingle your taste buds.

INGREDIENTS:

✦ medium sized sweet potatoes- 5

✦ cinnamon butter

✦ salted herb butter infused with garlic extracts

Serves: 4
Total Cook Time: 45-60 minutes
Temperature Setting: 450 degrees

DIRECTIONS:

1. Prick the surface of the sweet potatoes with a fork and place it on a foiled baking pan.

2. Bake the potatoes in the Nuwave Oven® for 45-60 minutes at 450 degrees and serve it with the two butters on the side.

Roasted Turkey with Garlic and Herbs

Thanksgiving is just around the corner and this recipe is the perfect one for you- it has you all covered for Thanksgiving lunch. All you need is a turkey and some herbs and you'll be good to go.

INGREDIENTS:

Serves: 4
Total Cook Time: 2.5 hours
Temperature Setting: 400 degrees

+ 6-pound turkey breast
+ 1 tsp. rosemary leaves crushed
+ ½ tsp. minced garlic
+ 1 tsp. thyme
+ ½ cup of softened butter
+ salt

DIRECTIONS:

1. Wash the turkey thoroughly with water and pat it dry.

2. Mix rosemary, butter, thyme, garlic, pepper, and salt in a bowl and rub the mixture onto the turkey.

3. Get the turkey into the Nuwave Oven® and cook it for 2.5 hours at 400 degrees until the internal temperature goes up to 180°F.

4. Remove the turkey from Nuwave and allow it to rest for some time before serving it.

Dinner
(Recipes)

Baked Sole and Asparagus

Fish and asparagus, you say? An interesting combo that tastes as lovely as it looks! This recipe is perfect for the nights when you're craving for something other than meat.

INGREDIENTS:

- ✦ 1/2 lb. asparagus, trimmed
- ✦ 3 tbsp. Parmesan cheese grated
- ✦ 1 tsp. olive oil
- ✦ 1/4 tsp. pepper
- ✦ 1/2 tsp. salt
- ✦ 1 tsp. chives, chopped
- ✦ 8 oz. sole
- ✦ 2 tbsp. breadcrumbs
- ✦ 1/4 lemon
- ✦ 2 tsp. mayonnaise

Serves: 2
Total Cook Time: 13-16 minutes
Temperature Setting: 450 degrees

DIRECTIONS:

1. Coat a shallow dish with nonstick spray.

2. Put asparagus into the dish, scatter salt, pepper and a drizzle of oil.

3. Mix bread crumbs and cheese in a bowl. Add pepper and salt to it.

4. In another bowl, mix chives, with the mayonnaise. Rub that onto the side of the fish.

5. Bake in the Nuwave Oven® for 13-16 minutes at 450 degrees.

6. Squeeze lemon juice onto the top of the fish once it has been cooked and plated.

Bacon Corn Muffins

There are many individuals who relish sweet muffins. However, we have here a savory one that could be equally delectable. Trust me, this recipe is absolutely simple!

INGREDIENTS:

✦ 1 and 1/4 cups of self-rising cornmeal mix
✦ 1/4 cup butter, melted
✦ 3/4 cup buttermilk
✦ 1 egg, beaten
✦ 1/3 cooked bacon, chopped

Serves: 6
Total Cook Time: 15-17 minutes
Temperature Setting: 425 degrees

DIRECTIONS:

1. Mix the cornmeal mix, bacon, buttermilk, egg and butter well in a bowl.

2. Pour this batter into a muffin pan that has been lightly greased. Make sure to only fill 3/4th way only.

3. Bake in the Nuwave Oven® for 15-17 minutes at 425 degrees.

4. Cool on wire rack for at least 10 minutes.

Boiled Chipotle Tilapia with Avocado Sauce

Avocado happens to be very versatile, fitting into breakfast, lunch, and dinner dishes with ease. Here is one such dinner recipe for you to live by. If you want some fish for dinner, it cannot get better than this.

INGREDIENTS:

- ✦ 1 peeled avocado, pitted
- ✦ 1/2 lb. tilapia
- ✦ 1 tsp. lime juice
- ✦ 1 tbsp. mayonnaise
- ✦ 1 tbsp. sour cream
- ✦ 2 and 1/2 tsp. chipotle
- ✦ cilantro chopped
- ✦ roasted garlic seasoning

Serves: 2
Total Cook Time: 10 minutes
Temperature Setting: 400 degrees

DIRECTIONS:

1. Put avocado, lime juice, seasoning and sour cream into a food processor and process well until creamy smooth.

2. Spray nonstick cooking spray on a baking pan.

3. Mix 1 tsp. seasoning and the mayonnaise together.

4. Coat the tilapia with the mayonnaise mixture.

5. Broil for 10 minutes in the Nuwave Oven® at 400 degrees.

6. Serve with the avocado sauce.

7. Garnish with cilantro and lime slices.

Cheesy Zucchini Squash Casserole

Are you a huge zucchini fan? Worry not, since we have a dinner recipe making use of just that! You're going to adore it!

INGREDIENTS:

- 1 lb. zucchini, sliced
- 1 sweet onion, sliced
- 1 lb. yellow squash, sliced
- 1 garlic clove, minced
- 1/2 cup sour cream
- 1 cup Swiss cheese, shredded
- 1 cup Cheddar cheese, shredded
- 1 large egg
- 1 tsp. salt
- 1 tsp. thyme
- 1/2 tsp. pepper
- 1 tbsp. butter, melted
- 3/4 cup panko crumbs seasoned

Serves: 12-14
Total Cook Time: 30-35 minutes
Temperature Setting: 350 degrees

DIRECTIONS:

1. Heat olive oil in a skillet. Add garlic and onion and cook for a couple of minutes.

2. Add the squash and the zucchini. Cook for 4 minutes.

3. Mix sour cream with beaten egg. Add the cheeses, salt, thyme, pepper, and the squash mixture into the egg mixture.

4. Pour entire mixture into a baking dish.

5. Stir melted butter and crumbs in a bowl and scatter over the mixture in the dish.

6. Bake in the Nuwave Oven® for 25-30 minutes at 350 degrees.

Baked Brie and Cranberry Bites

Don't be surprised if you end up gobbling down half of these once they come out of the Nuwave Oven®. This recipe is a win for those times you have guests at your house. Whether you want to put them out as snacks or appetizers, they're great!

INGREDIENTS:

+ 4 oz. triple crème brie
+ 4 sheets phyllo pastry sheets
+ 1/4 cup Cranberry Orange Relish
+ 1/4 cup butter, melted

Serves: 24
Total Cook Time: 10 minutes
Temperature Setting: 400 degrees

DIRECTIONS:

1. Cut the brie into slices.

2. Dampen phyllo sheets using a slightly damp towel. Butter each lightly and layer them one over the other.

3. Cut the sheets into 24 pieces. Place them into a muffin pan neatly.

4. Place a chunk of brie onto each phyllo sheet cup.

5. Put 1/2 tsp. of cranberry orange relish on top of each piece of brie.

6. Bake in the Nuwave Oven® for 8-10 minutes at 400 degrees.

Herb Roasted Garlic Turkey Breast

Turkey doesn't have to be just a Thanksgiving meal. You can make it in an easier way, and it is going to be just as tasty, with only a few steps. A light yet filling dish; this recipe takes no effort at all.

INGREDIENTS:

- 7 lb. turkey breast
- 1/2 tsp. garlic, minced
- 1 tsp. rosemary
- 1 tsp. ground thyme
- 1/2 cup butter
- salt
- pepper

Serves: 8
Total Cook Time: 2-4 hours
Temperature Setting: 180 degrees

DIRECTIONS:

1. Wash the turkey breast. Dry it and place it on a rack with breast side facing upwards.

2. Mix the thyme, salt, butter, rosemary, pepper, and garlic in a bowl. Rub it into the turkey.

3. Roast the turkey in the Nuwave Oven® for 2.5 hours at 180 degrees. Internal temperature should reach 180°F.

4. After cooking, allow meat to rest for 15 minutes, then carve.

Tortilla Pizza

Having a late-night pizza craving? Our tortilla pizza will cure that in a jiffy. Along with being delicious, this is one of the simplest dinner recipes out there.

INGREDIENTS:

+ mushrooms, sliced
+ grape tomatoes, sliced
+ red onion, sliced
+ 1 whole wheat tortilla
+ 1 oz. cheese blend
+ 1/4 cup marinara sauce

Serves: 1
Total Cook Time: 4 minutes
Temperature Setting: 425 degrees

DIRECTIONS:

1. On a piece of aluminum foil, place the tortilla.

2. Spread the marinara sauce evenly.

3. Sprinkle the topping generously.

4. Bake in the Nuwave Oven® for about 4 minutes at 425 degrees.

Open-Faced Tuna Melt

Many of us look for a sandwich to fill our tummy before bed. Grand and yum, this tuna melt will make you feel good as you devour it. This is perfect with English muffin halves or with regular toast too.

INGREDIENTS:

- 3 oz. white tuna, canned
- 2 tbsp. salsa
- 1 English muffin split
- 2 tbsp. cilantro, chopped
- 2 slices Colby-Jack cheese
- 1 tbsp. light mayonnaise

Serves: 1
Total Cook Time: 3 minutes
Temperature Setting: 350 degrees

DIRECTIONS:

1. Mix the tuna, mayonnaise, salsa and cilantro in a bowl.

2. Places the English muffin halves on a baking sheet. Put the cheese and tuna mixtures on top.

3. Bake in the Nuwave Oven® for 2-3 minutes at 350 degrees.

Moroccan Pork Kebabs

Browned and glazed, the kebabs are literally what you need to have, at least once in your lifetime. You could pile up some fried rice in a bowl or have these kebabs on its own. A mix of a number of ingredients, this recipe will become a favorite around the household.

INGREDIENTS:

Serves: 4
Total Cook Time: 45 minutes
Temperature Setting: 425 degrees

+ 1 and 1/2 oz. pork loin, boneless
+ 1 red onion
+ 1 eggplant
+ 1 half-pint tzatziki
+ pita bread
+ 2 tbsp. mint, chopped
+ 1/2 cucumber, sliced
+ 1/4 cup orange juice
+ 1 garlic clove, chopped
+ 4 tbsp. olive oil
+ 1 tbsp. tomato paste
+ 1 and 1/2 tsp. salt
+ 3/4 tsp. pepper
+ 1/8 tsp. ground cinnamon
+ 1 tbsp. ground cumin

DIRECTIONS:

1. Put the oil, orange juice, salt, pepper, cumin, tomato paste, cinnamon, garlic, and pork in a bowl. Mix and refrigerate from 30 minutes to 8 hours.

2. Add the salt, oil, and pepper to the onion and eggplant. Skewer them.

3. Bake them in the Nuwave Oven® for 20 minutes at 425 degrees.

4. Skewer the pork too. Add to the baking tray and bake for 20 minutes.

5. Put the bread over the pork and bake for another 5 minutes.

6. Add tzatziki, mint, and cucumber on the side and serve the dish.

Herb–Roasted Chicken Tenders

Without a doubt, you could enjoy a plate of my rendition of chicken tenders. While I love to devour this with an Arugula salad, you could have it on its own. Either way, the chicken tenders will be amazing, to say the least.

INGREDIENTS:

- ✦ 7 oz. chicken tenders
- ✦ 1/2 tbsp. herbs de Provence
- ✦ 1 tbsp. honey
- ✦ 1 tbsp. olive oil
- ✦ 2 tbsp. Dijon mustard
- ✦ salt
- ✦ pepper

Serves: 2
Total Cook Time: 8-10 minutes
Temperature Setting: 450 degrees

DIRECTIONS:

1. Pour half the oil on a tray.

2. Season the chicken with herbs de Provence, salt, and pepper. Put the chicken on the tray. Add honey and mustard on top.

3. Bake in the Nuwave Oven® for 8-10 minutes at 450 degrees.

4. Serve the chicken along with the sauce.

Baked Lasagna Toast

All of us find ourselves in the mood for some Italian treats every now and then, right? These baked toasts give you the true flavor of authentic Italian lasagna in a more lightweight recipe. You will not regret wolfing down a couple of them!

INGREDIENTS:

- 4 slices Italian bread
- 1 part ricotta cheese
- grated Pecorino Romano cheese
- 4 oz. mozzarella cheese
- 1 tbsp. olive oil
- 1 clove garlic
- 1 medium-sized zucchini
- 4 ripe plum tomatoes
- 4 tbsp. basil leaves, sliced
- pepper
- salt

Serves: 4
Total Cook Time: 15-17 minutes
Temperature Setting: 450 degrees

DIRECTIONS:

1. Toast the bread slices until golden.

2. Microwave the zucchini, oil, and garlic in a bowl for 4 minutes in the Nuwave Oven®.

3. Add the tomatoes, salt, and pepper in too. Microwave in the Nuwave for another 3 minutes.

4. Mix half the basil leaves, salt, pepper, ricotta, and Romano cheeses in a bowl.

5. Put bread slices on a plate. Spread 1/4 of cheese mixture on each. Put some of zucchini and tomato mixture on each. Finally, put mozzarella cheese on each slice.

6. Line a baking tray with aluminum foil. Toast bread in the Nuwave for 8-10 minutes at 450 degrees. Garnish with basil.

Oven Baked Fish and Chips

The following is a delectable option without the original fried elements. The twist to the classic is a win in my household. Definitely a healthier option when compared to the original, this Oven Baked Fish and Chips is delicious and filling.

INGREDIENTS:

✦ 4 pieces of Cod, 6 oz. each

✦ 1 Yukon gold or red potato, 3-4 lbs.

✦ 8 sprigs of thyme

✦ 1 lemon, sliced

✦ 4 tbsp. olive oil

✦ 1 clove of garlic, sliced

✦ 2 tbsp. capers

✦ salt

✦ pepper

Serves: 4
Total Cook Time: 38-47 minutes
Temperature Setting: 450 degrees

DIRECTIONS:

1. Put 2 tbsp. oil, salt, pepper, half the thyme, and potatoes on a baking tray. Bake in the Nuwave Oven® for 25-30 minutes at power level HI.

2. Cover the cod with garlic, lemon slices, salt, pepper, thyme, and sprinkle olive oil. Bake in the Nuwave for another 8-12 minutes at 450 degreees.

3. Take down the potatoes. On the tray, squeeze lemon juice. Bake again at 450 degrees for 5 minutes.

4. Pour the baked sauce over fish and potatoes.

Pesto Salmon

Healthy eating can't get any better than indulging in salmon fillets. Here's an easy recipe to relish! Preparing it will take no time at all.

INGREDIENTS:

- ✦ 1 and 1/4 oz. salmon
- ✦ 2 tbsp. pesto
- ✦ 1 lemon
- ✦ 2 tbsp. white wine
- ✦ 2 tbsp. pine nuts toasted

Serves: 4
Total Cook Time: 8-10 minutes
Temperature Setting: 375 degrees

DIRECTIONS:

1. Cover pan with aluminum foil and spray with oil. Place the salmon pieces, skin down.

2. Pour the lemon juice and white wine over the fish.

3. Wait for 15 minutes.

4. Spread the pesto over the salmons.

5. Broil in the Nuwave Oven® for 8-10 minutes at 375 degrees.

6. Garnish with lemon slices and pine nuts.

Banana Mini Meatloaves

Craving meatloaf, but don't have eggs around? Try this recipe instead! This is best for dinner, but could also be made for breakfast or lunch.

INGREDIENTS:

- 1 ripe banana
- 1 tsp. dried mustard
- 1 tsp. dried onion
- 1 tsp. hot sauce
- 1 tsp. Hungarian hot paprika
- little bit of whole wheat bread,
- 1/4 glass ketchup
- 1 tsp. salt
- 1 oz. ground beef
- 1 tsp. dried garlic
- 2 tbsp. Worcestershire sauce
- pepper

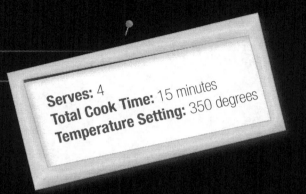

Serves: 4
Total Cook Time: 15 minutes
Temperature Setting: 350 degrees

DIRECTIONS:

1. Put the banana, salt, pepper, dried mustard, dried onion, the paprika, and dried garlic into a bowl and mash till smooth.

2. Put the bread into a food processor. Process till fine.

3. Add the banana mixture, the beef, mix well and then bake in the Nuwave Oven® at 350 degrees for 15 minutes.

Stuffed Mushrooms

Cheesy and light to the taste, these Stuffed Mushrooms are delicious all right. If you want something that is low in calories and manages to be creamy at the same time, this recipe is it. Our Stuffed Mushrooms will be a winner during dinner any day!

INGREDIENTS:

- 2 portabella mushroom caps
- 3 tbsp. olive oil
- 2 tbsp. ricotta cheese
- 2 garlic cloves
- 1/2 onion, chopped
- 1/2 cup tomatoes
- 6 oz. baby spinach
- 1/4 bread crumbs
- 1-2 tbsp. basil, chopped
- 1/4 cup Parmesan cheese
- salt
- pepper

Serves: 2
Total Cook Time: 20 minutes
Temperature Setting: 375 degrees

DIRECTIONS:

1. Scrape out the insides of the mushrooms.

2. In a pan, cook onion and garlic. Add spinach, ricotta cheese, tomatoes, basil, salt, and pepper.

3. Stuff the mushrooms with the pan contents. Grate Parmesan cheese over them.

4. Bake in the Nuwave Oven® for 20 minutes at 375 degrees.

Tandoori Chicken

A tangy Indian recipe like tandoori chicken is all that you need. This recipe will be a favorite, especially if you're into pita bread or naan. While conventional Tandoori Chicken requires you to marinade the chicken for hours, this recipe is as good, without the extra time. Beware of a large number of ingredients!

INGREDIENTS:

Serves: 4
Total Cook Time: 10 minutes
Temperature Setting: 200 degrees

- ✦ 4 chicken breasts
- ✦ 2 tbsp. chicken masala spice
- ✦ 1 garlic clove, crushed
- ✦ 1 tsp. ghee
- ✦ 1/2 lime
- ✦ salt

For the salad:
- ✦ cilantro, chopped
- ✦ 1/4 red cabbage, shredded
- ✦ 1/4 green cabbage, shredded
- ✦ 1/4 red onion, shredded
- ✦ 1/2 red pepper, shredded
- ✦ 1/2 yellow pepper, shredded
- ✦ cashews toasted

For the dressing:
- ✦ 1 tsp. ginger, minced
- ✦ 1 tsp. sesame oil
- ✦ 1 tsp. soy sauce

- ✦ 1 tsp. coconut milk
- ✦ 2 tsp. rice wine vinegar
- ✦ lime juice

DIRECTIONS:

1. Put the oil, chicken, salt, and the spices into a pan. Mix well and cook for 10 minutes in the Nuwave Oven® at 200 degrees.

2. After cooking, add the crushed garlic and lime juice on the chicken.

3. For the salad, mix all ingredients. Also mix up the ingredients for the dressing and pour it over the salad.

4. Give the entire thing a good stir.

Chicken Paillard

Paillard happens to be meat that is thinly pounded to allow even, stylish cooking. This chicken Paillard is far from an ordinary dinner recipe. Mouth-watering and simple at the same time, cooking this won't take much time.

INGREDIENTS:

✦ 1 chicken breast, boneless

✦ 1/4 cup olive oil

✦ 1/2 fennel bulb, shaved

✦ 1 garlic clove, sliced

✦ 1/4 cup mushroom, sliced

✦ 1 Roma tomato diced

✦ 1 and ½ tsp. capers

✦ 1 tbsp. parsley, chopped

✦ 2 tbsp. olives, sliced

✦ 2 sprigs thyme

✦ salt

✦ pepper

Serves: 1
Total Cook Time: 10-12 minutes
Temperature Setting: 400 degree

DIRECTIONS:

1. Line the baking tray with aluminum foil and brush olive oil.

2. Season the chicken with salt and pepper.

3. Mix the garlic, parsley, tomato, thyme, fennel, capers, mushrooms, salt, pepper, olives, and oil and pour over chicken

4. Bake in the Nuwave Oven® for 10-12 minutes at 400 degrees.

Tropical Chicken

A quick casserole-like dish, this chicken will leave you wanting more. This recipe is as groovy as it sounds, absolutely spot-on for dinner. Don't be surprised if you want a second and third helping!

INGREDIENTS:

+ 4 chicken breasts, boneless
+ 8 oz. canned pineapple, crushed
+ 2 tbsp. brown sugar
+ 2 tbsp. soy sauce
+ 1/8 tsp. ground ginger
+ 1/4 cup mustard
+ 1/4 cup cider vinegar

Serves: 4
Total Cook Time: 35-40 minutes
Temperature Setting: 350 degrees

DIRECTIONS:

1. Put the chicken into the baking pan or casserole dish.

2. Mix the rest of the ingredients and drizzle over chicken.

3. Bake in the Nuwave Oven® for 35-40 minutes at 350 degrees.

4. Serve with rice, if you want to.

Sweet or Savory Baked Sweet Potatoes

If you like to relish steaming sweet potatoes during the winter, you and I are very alike. This recipe is bound to be a favorite for obvious potato lovers. Simple and definitely filling, Sweet or Savory Baked Sweet Potatoes are just right for dinner.

INGREDIENTS:

- ✦ 6 sweet potatoes, medium-sized
- ✦ salted garlic herb butter
- ✦ cinnamon butter

Serves: 6
Total Cook Time: 45-60 minutes
Temperature Setting: 450 degrees

DIRECTIONS:

1. Line a baking pan with aluminum foil.

2. Prick the sweet potatoes with a fork a number of times. Place them on the pan.

3. Bake in the Nuwave Oven® for 45-60 minutes at 450 degrees.

4. Serve with either the cinnamon butter or salted garlic herb butter.

Hot Mexican Bean Dip

For parties or a game, chip and dip are a must! As with tortilla chips, this dip is guaranteed to be your new favorite Mexican recipe. I guarantee you that you won't feel otherwise.

INGREDIENTS:

- 30 oz. canned black beans
- 8 oz. Cheddar or Monterey Jack cheese
- 1/2 cup salsa
- 1/2 cup sour cream
- 1 tsp. hot pepper sauce

Serves: 8-10
Total Cook Time: 30 minutes
Temperature Setting: 350 degrees

DIRECTIONS:

1. Process the beans, salsa, half the cheese, hot pepper sauce, and sour cream in a food processor until you get a lumpy mixture.

2. Pour the mixture into 1-quart casserole dish.

3. Scatter the remaining cheese on top.

4. Bake in the Nuwave Oven® for 15 minutes at 350 degrees.

Desserts
[Recipes]

Smart Apple Tart

This certain apple tart works perfectly as a quick and healthy route to fully satisfy your cravings. It can also go great as an after dinner snack for one. This smart tart is not only quick but is also incredibly low fat for such a sweet dessert, and counts up to 150 calories.

INGREDIENTS:

+ 1 flour tortilla
+ ½ thin apple slices
+ 1 tsp. honey
+ 1 tsp. ground cinnamon

Serves: 1
Total Cook Time: 5 Minutes
Temperature Setting: 350 degrees

DIRECTIONS:

1. Thinly slice half of an apple or more if needed.

2. Place apple slices on the flour tortilla.

3. Generously drizzle apple slices with honey.

4. Sprinkle ground cinnamon over honey.

5. Fold up each corner of the tortilla to create an apple pie pouch and stick toothpicks on each corner to keep the tortilla in place.

6. Place the tart in the Nuwave Oven® and toast for 5 minutes until the apple slices are soft.

Drupe Crisps

If you're having a hard time making your loved ones eat healthy, then these stone-fruit mini crisps will come in handy. Having a hankering for something sweet? Even then, try these drupe crisps as they will make a great addition to your diet. The natural fruity goodness is sure to leave you satisfied.

INGREDIENTS:

Serves: 2
Total Cook Time: 40 Minutes
Temperature Setting: 350 degrees

- ½ cups sliced stone fruits
- ¼ cups sugar, divided
- ½ tsp cornstarch
- 3 tsp flour
- ¼ cinnamon
- pinch of salt
- 1.5 tsp butter, cold and cut into small pieces
- 3 tsp rolled oats

DIRECTIONS:

1. Whisk 1 tsp. sugar with cornstarch, sprinkle over fruit, and stir gently. Divide the fruit between two 8-ounce ramekins.

2. Combine flour, the rest of the sugar, salt, and butter in a bowl; use a fork to mix until crumbly. Stir in the oats and equally cover the fruit.

3. Bake in the Nuwave Oven® at 350 degrees for 40 minutes until fruit is cooked through.

4. Serve at room temperature with ice cream.

Oatmeal Cookies with Dry Grapes

Dry grapes, or raisins, can work as excellent additions to any home-made oatmeal cookies. Not only are they fantastic for livening the flavor, they are amazing desserts in their own rights. Even something as simple oatmeal cookies can make a special meal especially more special.

INGREDIENTS:

✦   1.5 tsp. baking powder, soda, kosher salt
✦   2 cups flour
✦   1 cup softened butter, sugar (also dark brown)
✦   2 tsp. vanilla
✦   2 eggs
✦   ½ cup dry grapes (raisins)
✦   3 cups non-instant oats

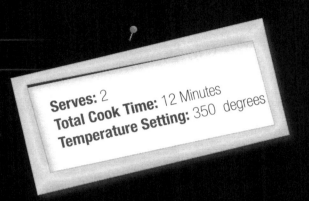

Serves: 2
Total Cook Time: 12 Minutes
Temperature Setting: 350 degrees

DIRECTIONS:

1.   Mix cream and sugar and stir the flour mixture.

2.   Put a hand mixer at high speed to beat into a light color.

3.   Add raisins and oats.

4.   Fill cookie scoop and raise the dough level, dropping on the baking sheet and bake in the Nuwave Oven® at 350 degrees for about 12 minutes.

5.   A golden color should arise with cracks.

6.   Give two minutes to cool down.

Rum-Spiked Caramel Mango

Mango, while being sweet by itself, is a great fruit to eat. It can be made even better by adding rum and caramel into a wonderful, sweet combination. Such amazing combinations can make one realize just how versatile mango is as a stand-alone ingredient.

INGREDIENTS:

+ 2 mangoes
+ ½ cup sugar, water, vanilla bean
+ 8 to 10 green cardamom pods
+ ¼ cup rum

Serves: 1
Total Cook Time: 12-13 Minutes
Temperature Setting: 350 degrees

DIRECTIONS:

1. Peel mangoes and then cut them into slices.

2. Scrape out the vanilla beans and stir with cardamom pods. Cook this mixture in the Nuwave Oven® at a HI power level for 5 minutes and add rum afterward.

3. Recook in the Nuwave, making sure to melt away the rum and caramel for 2 minutes at 350 degrees. For a lighter caramel sauce, add a mango and cook for 3 minutes more.

4. Roast in the Nuwave at HI for 5 minutes to bubble the juices.

5. Sea salt can boost the taste.

Grilled Banana S'mores

Escape to your childhood summer camp days with this quick and fun dessert snack. It is the perfect pick-me-up snack for the weekends. It is also suitable as a snack on the go, meaning that you can bunch on this deliciousness basically anytime you want.

INGREDIENTS:

- ✦ 1 banana, peeled
- ✦ 2 tbsp. miniature marshmallows
- ✦ 1 tbsp. chocolate chips
- ✦ 1 tbsp. cereal, slightly crushed
- ✦ 1 rectangular cut aluminum foil

Serves: 1
Total Cook Time: 4-5 Minutes
Temperature Setting: 400 degrees

DIRECTIONS:

1. Slice the banana lengthwise, somewhat open, and place it on the foil.

2. Put marshmallows and chocolate chips into the banana.

3. Wrap banana in foil and grill in the Nuwave Oven® for 4-5 minutes at 400 degrees until the marshmallows soften.

4. Unwrap the foil and sprinkle crushed cereal of your choice.

Peanut Butter Cookies

Who doesn't know peanut butter cookies? They are the epitome of after lunch snack. This is the type of light food that can be eaten anywhere. Easy to store in all temperatures, and tastes great; peanut butter cookies are truly important sweets.

INGREDIENTS:

- ✦ 2 tbsp. flour
- ✦ 1/16 tsp. baking soda
- ✦ 1/16 tsp. salt
- ✦ 1.5 tbsp. peanut butter
- ✦ ¼ tsp. vanilla extract
- ✦ 1.5 tbsp. maple syrup
- ✦ 1 tsp. applesauce

Serves: 1
Total Cook Time: 10 Minutes
Temperature Setting: 350 degrees

DIRECTIONS:

1. Mix the flour, salt, vanilla, and the dry ingredients together.

2. Add baking soda and the butter to form a new mixture, flatten to create cookie shapes.

3. Baking in the Nuwave Oven® for about 10 minutes at 350 degrees should suffice.

4. Use sugar for more chewiness.

Baked S'mores

It's Mid-July and you have a sudden hankering for some authentic, smooth, chocolatey s'mores. Unfortunately, as a working class adult you don't always have time to build a fire for those s'mores. This is why you should know that; you don't always need a campfire to snack on some old fashioned s'mores!

INGREDIENTS:

✦ 1 cup chocolate chips
✦ 8/9 large marshmallows, cut in half
✦ 1 pack of graham crackers

Serves: 2
Total Cook Time: 4-5 Minutes
Temperature Setting: 400 degrees

DIRECTIONS:

1. In a cast iron skillet, add the chocolate chips and neatly cover the chocolate chips with the marshmallows.

2. Place the skillet in the Nuwave Oven® at 400 degrees and cook for 4-5 minutes.

3. Serve with graham crackers for scooping or slightly crush them to put on top.

Baked Granny Smith Apples

Granny Smith apples don't only look good, they taste amazing and are super juicy too. They are perfect for making tarts so give them a try whenever you can. Remember, an apple a day keeps the doctor away; so if you are looking for natural healthiness, these apples are among the best you can select.

INGREDIENTS:

+ ½ apples, 6 sliced pieces
+ ½ tbsp. molasses
+ ½ tbsp. flax seed
+ cinnamon and walnuts

Serves: 1
Total Cook Time: 30 Minutes
Temperature Setting: 400 degrees

DIRECTIONS:

1. Use a baking sheet and arrange apples in equal shapes.

2. Bake in the Nuwave Oven® for 25 minutes at 400 degrees.

3. Add toasted walnuts and bake for another 5 minutes at HI.

4. After cooking, add cinnamon sprinkles and molasses for flavor.

5. Add flax seeds to form the basic taste.

Raisin Cookies with Spices

We all know how raisin and spices can go together to make tasty cookies. Especially with interesting ingredients such as ground flax and coconut oil, the combinations of cookies can be endless. For a light snack, a simple contortion of raisin and spices can go a long way in achieving the ultimate dessert.

INGREDIENTS:

- ✦ 2 tbsp. ground flax
- ✦ 2 tbsp. coconut oil
- ✦ 4 tbsp. water
- ✦ ½ tsp. baking soda
- ✦ 2 cups almond flour
- ✦ ¼ cup honey
- ✦ ¼ tsp. cloves, nutmeg, ginger
- ✦ 1/3 cup raisins

Serves: 1
Total Cook Time: 30 Minutes
Temperature Setting: 350 degrees

DIRECTIONS:

1. Mix ground flax with water and then thicken in one bowl. Mix flour, oil, and honey in another.

2. Stir and add baking soda, raisins, and spices; mix thoroughly.

3. In an 8 x 8 pan, form bars by pressing the dough with the bottom surface.

4. Bake the dough for 30 minutes in the Nuwave Oven® at 350 degrees.

Baked Mascarpone Figs

Figs have never achieved the spotlight they deserve. But with this sweet recipe you'll forget all about Fig Newton. Baked Mascarpone figs are just what you would need to finish an amazing meal, and enjoy an excellent dessert.

INGREDIENTS:

✦   4 fresh Figs

✦   80g Mascarpone

✦   Ground Cinnamon

✦   4 tsp. Honey

Serves: 6
Total Cook Time: 10 Minutes
Temperature Setting: 400 degrees

DIRECTIONS:

1.   Cut the Figs into four pieces and leave the base attached to hold the fruit in one piece.

2.   Grease a tray with oil, so it doesn't stick and assemble your figs on it.

3.   Drizzle 1 tsp. of honey onto each piece of the fig and put a spoonful of mascarpone into the base of each fig using a spoon and sprinkle ground cinnamon on top.

4.   Bake in the Nuwave Oven® for 10 minutes at 400 degrees and spread the honey that topped the figs before it caramelizes.

Buttermilk Surprise

Having a hard time deciding what cake to bake for a kid's party? Well, your concern is quite common, as kids have very specific taste for desserts. A good old surprise can definitely shake things up in a good way, and better yet, add buttermilk in the mixture for creamy goodness.

INGREDIENTS:

+ 1 ½ cups of flour
+ ½ baking soda
+ ¼ teaspoon salt
+ ½ cup softened butter
+ 1 cup sugar
+ 1 teaspoon extract of vanilla
+ 1 egg
+ ¾ cup buttermilk
+ ¼ multicolored sprinkles
+ frosting of cream cheese

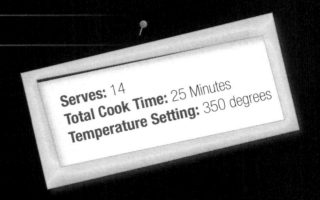

Serves: 14
Total Cook Time: 25 Minutes
Temperature Setting: 350 degrees

DIRECTIONS:

1. Grease two 8-inch cake pans and line with parchment paper.

2. Combine butter, sugar, and vanilla extract, and using an electrical mixer on high speed, beat and add eggs one at a time until frothy.

3. Add flour mix and buttermilk and stir ¼ cup of sprinkles.

4. Divide batter evenly on each pan, place it in the Nuwave Oven®, and bake for 25 minutes at 350 degrees until it softens. To check, insert a toothpick and see if it comes out clean.

5. Cool to room temp before removing from pan.

Pecan Honey Bundt

Any cook would agree that a simple Bundt cake is the perfect gift to bring to a dinner party. Even outside a formal occasion, Bundt cakes are amazing as they not only look nice, they taste nice as well. Surely, this niceness is something you would want to master properly.

INGREDIENTS:

- ½ cup brown sugar
- ½ cup sugar
- ½ cup pecans
- 2 tsp. ground cinnamon
- 18.25 ounce cake mix
- 2/3 cup vegetable oil
- 4 eggs
- 8 oz. plain yogurt
- 1 tsp. butter

Serves: 11
Total Cook Time: 55 Minutes
Temperature Setting: 350 degrees

DIRECTIONS:

1. Grease the sides of the Bundt pan with butter and sprinkle flour.

2. Combine cake mix, oil, eggs, and yogurt and beat with a mixer on standard speed for 2 minutes.

3. In a separate bowl, mix brown sugar, normal sugar, pecans, and cinnamon until blended.

4. Spread half the batter in the pan, spread the cinnamon mix, and cover with the rest of the batter.

5. Bake in the Nuwave Oven® for 55 minutes at 350 degrees, until the toothpick that has been inserted, comes out clean.

6. Allow cake to cool for 10 minutes before serving.

Chocolate Chip Cookies

This is the standard, yet an essential sweet snack of all time. Making perfect cookies may be difficult, but a standard one is just as good. Keep in mind that chocolate chip cookies are basically the backbone of crunchy desserts so learning how to bake them properly is something every chef must undertake.

INGREDIENTS:

+ 1 stick of non-salty butter
+ ¾ dark brown sugar, regular sugar
+ 2 eggs
+ 1 tsp. vanilla extract
+ 12 ounces chocolate chunks
+ ½ cup flour
+ ¾ baking soda
+ 1 tsp. salt

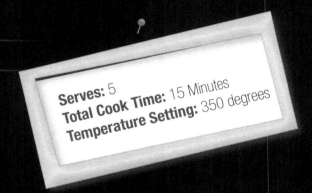

Serves: 5
Total Cook Time: 15 Minutes
Temperature Setting: 350 degrees

DIRECTIONS:

1. Line two baking sheets with silicone sheets.

2. Place butter in Nuwave Oven® for a minute till it melts.

3. Combine vanilla, eggs, and sugars with this butter by whisking.

4. In another bowl, whisk flour with salt and baking soda.

5. Stir the contents of the two bowls together and add in the chocolate chips.

6. Roll the dough and form shapes of the cookies, and bake in the Nuwave at 350 degrees for about 15 minutes to get the crispiness.

Grapefruit with broiled molten sugar

Grapefruits are can be pretty sour, but for an effective dessert, many prefer sweetened grapefruits. Broiling makes them healthier consumables. Adding molten sugar makes them tastier than ever before. You simply cannot pass up this combination of natural sweetness.

INGREDIENTS:

+ ½ grapefruit, preferably sweet and red
+ 2 tsp. brown sugar
+ 2 tbsp. granulated sugar
+ sea salt and mint

Serves: 1
Total Cook Time: 5 Minutes
Temperature Setting: 500 degrees

DIRECTIONS:

1. Combine the two sugars in a bowl.

2. Sprinkle the sugar mixture on the exposed parts of the grapefruit.

3. Melt the sugars using a torch and broil in the Nuwave Oven® for about 5 minutes at 500 degrees.

4. Garnish and mint can be added for better taste.

Roasted Persimmon Slices

Persimmons may seem like simple fruits at first, but the variety of ways in which they can be used is astonishing. Simply roasting them with the right spices creates innovativeness. Slices of persimmons are amazingly sweet and can be served as mouth-watering desserts.

INGREDIENTS:

- ✦ 2 Fuyu persimmons
- ✦ spices such as crystallized ginger and cardamom
- ✦ additional spices like nutmeg, 5-spice, and paprika
- ✦ chili flakes

Serves: 1
Total Cook Time: 10 Minutes
Temperature Setting: 400 degrees

DIRECTIONS:

1. Slice persimmons to halves.

2. Place the cut fruits on parchment or foil.

3. Sprinkle the spices over the fruits.

4. Roast in the Nuwave Oven® for 5 minutes at 400 degrees.

5. Blue cheese can be added with paprika for a more enhanced flavor.

Oven-baked Bananas

Getting easily tired of certain fruits is very common when you're on a routine diet. With the help of this quick and certainly low fat recipe, spicing up your mundane diet will be a breeze. You don't have to worry about controlling your diet and getting the right nutrients since these bananas are jam-packed with energy.

INGREDIENTS:

✦ 1 ripe banana sliced lengthwise

✦ 2 tbsp. lemon juice

✦ ground cinnamon

✦ 2 tbsp. honey

✦ dark chocolate chips (optional)

Serves: 1
Total Cook Time: 10 Minutes
Temperature Setting: 350 degrees

DIRECTIONS:

1. Line a tray in the Nuwave Oven® with non-stick aluminum foil.

2. Drizzle or brush banana halves with lemon juice and sprinkle with cinnamon.

3. Place it in the Nuwave and bake for 10 minutes at 350 degrees.

4. After cooling down, cut into 1-inch pieces and add the chocolate chips if desired.

Baked Crispy Apples

Apples are downright delicious when used in the right way. Using the Nuwave Oven®, it is possible to add ingredients to bake them into crispy edibles. These treats can be used as mouthwatering dessert items that can satisfy both the stomach and the taste buds.

INGREDIENTS:

+ 4 apples, medium size
+ ½ tsp lemon juice, cinnamon
+ ½ tbsp. flour
+ 2 tbsp. brown sugar
+ 1 tsp. butter, unsalted
+ 2 tsp. water

Serves: 1
Total Cook Time: 35 Minutes
Temperature Setting: 350 degrees

DIRECTIONS:

1. Chop apples and add brown sugar, cinnamon, and lemon juice.

2. Add flour and granola with the leftovers of the initial ingredients.

3. Sprinkle water and put in a bit of butter.

4. Bake in the Nuwave at 350 degrees until a brown color has been formed. This takes about 35 minutes usually.

Toasted Dehydrated Apples

The Nuwave Oven® is amazing in the sense that it can create a multitude of different items, in addition to being able to dehydrate fruits. Toasted, dehydrated apples can be prepared easily in this machine. It is a good idea to test out your new Nuwave by following this recipe.

INGREDIENTS:

✦ apples (big, red, and juicy)
✦ lemon juice water mixture
✦ sugar

Serves: 1
Total Cook Time: 1.5 hours
Temperature Setting: 200 degrees

DIRECTIONS:

1. Cut the apples and take out the cores. Keep the peel for more nutritional value.

2. Lemon juice water mixture can sustain the dehydration.

3. Spread them out on the cooking rack and dehydrate at 200 degrees, each side for 45 minutes. You may repeat this process depending on the amount of the pieces.

4. Add a bit of sugar if the taste doesn't feel right. Otherwise, you're done when the cut pieces are toasted and crispy.

Loaf o' Bananas

Simply known as the banana bread, this dessert equivalent of garlic bread is known around the world. The recipe to create these has been said to be passed down from generations, though nearly nothing can beat the modern style of preparing them. For a fun dessert, try this banana bread.

INGREDIENTS:

✦ 1 pack (517g) white cake mix
✦ 1 cup ripe bananas, mashed
✦ ½ cup buttermilk
✦ 1/3 cup vegetable oil
✦ 3 eggs, beaten
✦ 1 cup nuts, chopped
✦ 1 tsp. butter

Serves: 6
Total Cook Time: 40 Minutes
Temperature Setting: 350 degrees

DIRECTIONS:

1. Grease two loaf pans (9x5x3) with butter and then slightly coat with flour.

2. Combine cake mix, bananas, buttermilk, oil, and eggs and beat it with a mixer on standard speed for 2 minutes.

3. Mix in nuts and pour into prepared pans.

4. Bake in the Nuwave Oven® for 40 minutes at 350 degrees and to check, insert a toothpick and see if it comes out clean.

5. Cool for 10 minutes before removing from the pan.

Coco Soufflé Cake

Soufflé cakes are any chef's nightmare, considering how easily it can go wrong. That being said, we can't deny the brilliance of a perfectly executed soufflé. So it is of utmost importance for any serious chef to get the preparation methods right to the point.

INGREDIENTS:

- 2 tbsp. unsalted butter, chopped
- 8 ounces dark chocolate
- 9 eggs, separated
- 1 ¼ cups granulated sugar
- 2 egg whites
- 1 tbsp. water
- 1 pinch salt
- 1 cup flour
- 1 cup fresh fruit

Serves: 16
Total Cook Time: 35 Minutes
Temperature Setting: 475 degrees

DIRECTIONS:

1. Grease a 10x3-inch round pan with butter and line the pan's bottom with parchment paper, sprinkling the pan except the edge.

2. Add 2 tbsp. of butter and chocolate. Stir until meltdown.

3. Combine egg yolks and sugar and mix for two minutes. Add chocolate afterward.

4. Whip all the egg whites, salt, and water until the foam occurs.

5. Add the remaining sugar and meringue to the chocolate mixture and flour.

6. Bake at 375 degrees in the Nuwave Oven® for around 35 minutes and add fruits in the end.

Sides and Snacks (Recipes)

Freshly Toasted Nuts

Freshly toasted nuts are delicious, crunchy little goodies that will have us craving them over and over again! Add to cereals or desserts. Have them at your convenience.

INGREDIENTS:

Total Cook Time: 10 minutes
Temperature Setting: 350 degrees

* any amount of preferred nuts
* cooking oil, neutral oil (i.e. grapeseed) or nut oils

DIRECTIONS:

1. Spread nuts evenly over baking sheet.

2. Drizzle some oil over the nuts and toss to make sure all of it is covered. Make sure not to use too much, this can cause burning.

3. Toast: Put in the Nuwave Oven® for 5-10 minutes at 350 degrees.

4. Remove the nuts every 5 minutes and stir to avoid over-heating. (Don't allow the color to become dark brown).

5. Start cooling the nuts immediately by moving them to a different tray.

Za'atar Pita Chips & Yogurt Dip Combination

Za'atar pita chips mixed with a yogurt dip will leave your stomach yearning for more. Za'atar is a Middle Eastern yogurt known worldwide. Enjoy with family and friends.

INGREDIENTS:

✦ 4 tablespoons of Za'atar
✦ 2 large pitas
✦ 1/8th teaspoon salt
✦ 5 tablespoons olive oil
✦ 1 cup plain yogurt (Greek yogurt)
✦ 1 small garlic clove, minced or grated
✦ 1 tablespoon chopped mint

Total Cook Time: 5 to 7 minutes
Temperature Setting: 350 degrees

DIRECTIONS:

1. Mix Za'atar and olive oil together in a small bowl and form a paste.

2. Cut open one pita by cutting around the edge (makes two rounds).

3. Repeat with remaining pita.

4. Put the pita rounds on a baking sheet after spreading the Za'atar mixture on the rough sides of the pita rounds (use the back side of a spoon).

5. Bake in the Nuwave Oven® until edges are golden for 5-7 minutes at 350 degrees.

6. Cool off the pita before cutting into wedges.

7. Mix yogurt, garlic, mint, and salt. Serve with pita chips.

Healthy & Crispy Oven-Toasted Kale Chips

Need to munch on something that's just healthy and high in fiber? Don't want it affecting your weight or cholesterol? This is the recipe for you!

INGREDIENTS:

✦ bite size pieces of kale

✦ coconut oil

✦ salt

✦ pepper

✦ garlic powder

Total Cook Time: 2-4 minutes
Temperature Setting: 350 degrees

DIRECTIONS:

1. Take the kale and wash (if necessary).

2. Cut the kale into small pieces and place on a tray.

3. Sprinkle some coconut oil, pepper, garlic powder, and salt on top.

4. Toast the kale in the Nuwave Oven® at 350 degrees for 2-5 minutes or until the edges become brown and crunchy. Enjoy!

Yummy Baked Sweet Potatoes or Yams

Baked potatoes are a favorite in many households. Potato recipes come in a wide variety. Here's a simple potato recipe you have to try out. Enjoy creamily and crispy baked sweet potatoes!

INGREDIENTS:

✦ 3-4 pieces of sweet potatoes or yams
✦ melted coconut or vegetable oil

Total Cook Time: 45-60 minutes
Temperature Setting: 400 degrees

DIRECTIONS:

1. Coat sweet potatoes/yams with melted coconut oil or vegetable oil.

2. Place on the baking tray.

3. Bake potatoes/yams in the Nuwave Oven® for 45-60 minutes at 400 degrees, until baked slightly brown. Remember not to wrap the potatoes in foil until you finish baking.

Toasted Potatoes

Toasted potatoes is a must taste for potato lovers. With the wide variety of potato related recipes out there, this one's a simple yet yummy one. Enjoy delicious roasted potatoes for lunch or dinner.

INGREDIENTS:

+ baby potatoes or large potatoes cut up into 1 square inch sized
+ olive oil
+ salt
+ pepper
+ herbs

Total Cook Time: 25 minutes
Temperature Setting: 400 degrees

DIRECTIONS:

1. Cut the potatoes into 1 square inch in size if you are using large potatoes.

2. Toss your potatoes with 2-3 tablespoons of olive oil, pepper, salt, and your choice of herbs.

3. Bake in the Nuwave Oven® for 25 minutes at 400 degrees. Or until the potatoes are cooked and sizzling. Stir the potatoes at least once in order to ensure browning.

Crispy Parmesan Zucchini

Not a zucchini fan? This recipe might just make you become one! Crunch away on crispy pieces of Parmesan Zucchini.

INGREDIENTS:

- ✦ 4 zucchini cut lengthwise, quartered
- ✦ 1/2 cup Parmesan (grated)
- ✦ 1/2 teaspoon oregano (dried)
- ✦ 1/2 teaspoon thyme (dried)
- ✦ 1/4 teaspoon garlic powder
- ✦ 1/2 teaspoon dried basil
- ✦ salt
- ✦ black pepper
- ✦ 2 tablespoons olive oil
- ✦ 2 tablespoons fresh parsley (chopped)

Total Cook Time: 15-20 minutes
Temperature Setting: 400 degrees

DIRECTIONS:

1. Mix in a small bowl thyme, Parmesan, oregano, garlic powder, basil, pepper, and salt (to taste).

2. Drizzle olive oil and add the Parmesan mixture.

3. Bake in the Nuwave Oven® at 400 degrees for about 15-20 minutes until they look crispy and golden brown.

4. Serve garnished with parsley (optional).

Delicious Toasted Cornbread

Cornbread is used in all sorts of dishes. This delicious recipe will have you wondering why you didn't try it before. Simple yet delicious.

INGREDIENTS:

- 1 1/2 cups Quaker oatmeal (old fashioned)
- 1 cup yellow cornmeal
- 1 egg (large)
- 1/4 cup granulated sugar
- 1/4 teaspoon Salt
- 1 cup soy milk
- 1 large egg
- 2 teaspoons baking powder
- 1/2 cup applesauce, unsweetened
- 1/4 teaspoon chili powder (optional)

Total Cook Time: 20 minutes
Temperature Setting: 400 degrees

DIRECTIONS:

1. Put oatmeal into a food processor or blender until it becomes a powder.

2. Mix and stir the powdered cornmeal with sugar, baking powder, and salt.

3. Add applesauce, soymilk, and egg and mix until properly blended.

4. Add in chili powder (optional).

5. Pour mixture into the Nuwave Oven® pan and bake at 400 degrees for 20 minutes.

Cheesy Tomato Crackers

Love munching on crackers? Wish you could keep enjoying them throughout the day? Here's a whole new way of baking crackers!

INGREDIENTS:

+ 4 slices fresh tomato
+ 2 whole grain crackers (large size)
+ 1-ounce cheese (cheddar or preferred cheese)
+ salt (optional)

Total Cook Time: 1 minute
Temperature Setting: 425 degrees

DIRECTIONS:

1. Place your crackers on a cookie sheet and put the tomato pieces on top.

2. Sprinkle salt on top of tomatoes (optional).

3. Cut thin slices of the cheese and put on top.

4. Place in the Nuwave Oven® and microwave for about a minute and allow the cheese to melt.

5. Take out the crackers and munch away!

Oven Roasted Balsamic Tomatoes

Enjoy fresh roasted balsamic tomatoes from the comfort of your own home. A great dish for vegetarians and meat lovers alike. Can be used as a side with heavy meals.

INGREDIENTS:

✦ 10 large vine tomatoes (halved)

✦ 4 sliced garlic cloves

✦ thyme

✦ 2 tablespoons olive oil

✦ 3 tablespoons balsamic vinegar

Total Cook Time: 45 minutes
Temperature Setting: 425 degrees

DIRECTIONS:

1. Place tomatoes on the baking sheet.

2. Add thyme and garlic.

3. Drizzle olive oil and balsamic vinegar.

4. Add seasoning of choice.

5. Roast in the Nuwave Oven® at 425 degrees for 45 minutes.

Baked Beans with Beef

Beans are a favorite in lots of households worldwide. They have you craving them over and over. But as they say, you haven't tried beans until you've tasted Boston Baked Beans!

INGREDIENTS:

- 2 cups beans
- ½ pound beef
- 1 onion (sliced)
- 3 tablespoons molasses
- ¼ teaspoon black pepper
- ¼ teaspoon salt and dry mustard
- ¼ cup sugar (preferably brown)
- ½ cup ketchup
- 2 teaspoons salt

Total Cook Time: 1.5-2.25 hours
Temperature Setting: 325 degrees

DIRECTIONS:

1. Soak the navy beans overnight in cold water.

2. Simmer beans in this water until they become tender (1-2 hours).

3. Drain and set aside this water for later.

4. Put beans in a 2-quart pot of beans or casserole dish; place beans in the bottom and layer with beef and onion.

5. Combine in a saucepan molasses, pepper, salt, dry mustard, ketchup, sauce and brown sugar.

6. Pour some of the leftover water on the beans.

7. Cover the dish with foil paper.

8. Bake for 1.5 hours to 2.25 hours in the Nuwave Oven® at 325 degrees until the beans become tender (add more liquid halfway through if necessary, to avoid drying).

Rosemary Roasted Bananas

Here's a unique recipe that doesn't require too many ingredients. Make yourself this finger-licking dessert that can be used as a garnish for meat meals. Or you can have them on one of those 'dessert-craving' days.

INGREDIENTS:

- 3 finger bananas
- fresh rosemary leaves
- butter (softened)
- maple syrup
- salt
- black pepper

Total Cook Time: 3-4 minutes
Temperature Setting: 425 degrees

DIRECTIONS:

1. Cover the baking pan with aluminum foil or baking paper.

2. Coat the baking paper with butter.

3. Cut bananas lengthwise into halves.

4. Place bananas on the baking sheet and sprinkle with salt and black pepper.

5. Brush bananas with soft butter and a thin layer of maple syrup.

6. Add a few rosemary leaves on top of each of the bananas (not chopped).

7. Bake at 425 degrees in the Nuwave Oven® for 3-4 minutes.

Crunchy Toasted Pine Nuts

INGREDIENTS:

+ any amount of pine nuts
+ cooking oil or nut oils

Total Cook Time: 5-10 minutes
Temperature Setting: 350 degrees

DIRECTIONS:

1. Over a baking sheet, spread out the nuts evenly.

2. Drizzle some oil over the nuts and toss to make sure all of it is covered. Make sure not to use too much, this can cause burning.

3. Bake: Put in the Nuwave Oven® for 5-10 minutes at 350 degrees. You can pause every 2 or 3 minutes to stir the nuts in order to avoid overheating.

Cheese Dip Pimentos with Spices

This is a recipe for cheese lovers. A spicy, cheesy dip that you can do anytime, for anyone. Add it onto your all-time favorite dips.

INGREDIENTS:

- ✦ 1 jar (4 oz.) sweet pimentos, drained
- ✦ 8 ounces cream cheese
- ✦ 8-ounce block of cheddar cheese, shredded
- ✦ 1/4 cup chopped onion
- ✦ 2 teaspoons jarred garlic (or 2 whole cloves)
- ✦ 1/2 cup mayonnaise
- ✦ 1/2 teaspoon pepper and salt
- ✦ 2 tablespoons sauce (hot)

Total Cook Time: 40-45 minutes
Temperature Setting: 350 degrees

DIRECTIONS:

1. Combine all ingredients in a bowl.

2. Mix using a hand mixer, hand blender or food mixer.

3. Bake: Place in the Nuwave Oven® for 40-45 minutes at 350 degrees (until the edges become golden brown).

Cheesy Ham Toast with Garlic Spread

Served extensively at the bakeries of Germany, this rustic and traditional delicacy is a sure crowd pleaser. With good quality bread, a great garlic spread, and cheese; this recipe takes approximately ten minutes to prepare. Best served hot, enjoy the authentic German taste at home with this beautiful toast.

INGREDIENTS:

✦ 2 pieces Italian bread

✦ ¼ lbs. diced ham, sautéed in butter

✦ 2 tbsp garlic spread

✦ Parmesan cheese, flaked

✦ Cheddar cheese, shredded

Serves: 4
Total Cook Time: 5 to 10 minutes
Temperature Setting: 400 degree

DIRECTIONS:

1. Slice the two pieces of bread into half, yielding four pieces in total

2. Placing the slices on an oven proof tray, spoon over the garlic spread and diced ham over each

3. Sprinkle parmesan cheese and sharp cheddar cheese on top of each slice

4. In the Nuwave Oven®, toast the bread at 400 degrees for 5-10 minutes till the cheese has melted.

Roasted Tomato Corn Fritters with Lime Aioli

Corn fritters are great snacks for the whole family and can be customized in any way you want. With your Nuwave Oven®, you can take these fritters to a new level by roasting the tomatoes in it. The lime aioli adds a dash of tanginess to the dish.

INGREDIENTS:

- ✦ 4 tomatoes, cut in half
- ✦ 2 tsp olive oil
- ✦ ½ tsp black pepper
- ✦ ½ cup flour
- ✦ 1 tsp baking powder
- ✦ 1/3 cup milk
- ✦ 1 beaten egg
- ✦ 1 ½ cup corn kernels from 3 ears
- ✦ ⅓ cup spring onions, finely chopped
- ✦ ¼ tsp salt
- ✦ 3 tbsp. mayonnaise
- ✦ 2 tbsp. lime juice
- ✦ ½ clove of garlic, minced
- ✦ 1 tsp water, cold
- ✦ 4 cup arugula, loosely packed
- ✦ 4 slice prosciutto, ¼ oz.

Serves: 4
Total Cook Time: 1 hour 35 minutes
Temperature Setting: 375 degrees

DIRECTIONS:

1. On a baking sheet, place the tomato halves side up. Sprinkle 1 tsp oil and ¼ tsp black pepper. Bake in Nuwave at 375 degrees till tomatoes are soft and devoid of moisture.

2. In a mixing bowl, combine flour, baking powder, milk, and eggs, and stir till the mixture is smooth. Add in the remaining pepper, onions, salt, and corn.

3. Heating ½ tsp oil in a skillet over medium heat, spoon the batter to make six fritters. Cook till the edges are golden. Turn the fritters over and cook similarly for two minutes.

4. To prepare lemon aioli, mix the lemon juice, garlic, water, and mayonnaise.

5. Top each fritter with one tomato slice and arugula. Repeat the layers similarly with fritters, arugula and again fritters on top. Garnish each with one prosciutto slice and drizzle with aioli.

Crispy Korean Fried Chicken

This beautiful Korean recipe is nothing like the chicken served in your local fast food joint. The crisp is wholesome with a light layer of starch and the sweet sauce tantalizes just the right taste buds. Why not try a different fried chicken this season?

INGREDIENTS:

- 900 gm chicken wings
- 3 tbsp. brown sugar
- 1 tbsp. Korean sweet chili paste (gochujang)
- ½ tsp salt
- 1 tsp soy sauce
- 1/3 cup Korean liquor (soju)
- 2 tbsp. grated ginger
- 3 cloves garlic, grated
- 1 tsp sesame oil
- 1 tsp potato starch
- 1 tsp sesame seeds
- Oil for frying
- Korean chili pepper (gochugaru) to taste

Serves: 4
Total Cook Time: 30 minutes
Temperature Setting: 450 degrees

DIRECTIONS:

1. Sprinkling salt over the chicken wings, cover them with a plastic wrap and put them in the fridge for a day.

2. To make the sweet sauce, mix brown sugar, sweet chili paste, Korean liquor, soy sauce, ginger, garlic and sesame oil. Boil the mixture until thickened. Add chili pepper till it's as spicy as you want. Strain the sauce in fine sieve.

3. Taking the chicken out of the fridge, coat each wing with a thin layer of potato starch.

4. Set your Nuwave Oven® to 450 degrees, bake the wings for 15 minutes and flip the other side to bake for another 15 minutes. Remove and let rest for 5 minutes

5. As soon as you remove the pieces, toss them in the sauce to get them evenly coated. Make sure they do not sit in the sauce for long.

Quick and Easy Greek Frittata

It might sound pretty grandiose to prepare frittata at home, however, it isn't! Exotic flavours, rich texture and wholesome goodness of vegetables make it a very healthy and filling breakfast. Try this fool-proof, hassle free recipe of this Greek classic that you can share with your family.

INGREDIENTS:

- ✦ 8 oz. Feta cheese, crumbled
- ✦ 3 tbsp. olive oil
- ✦ 2 tsp kosher salt
- ✦ 10 eggs
- ✦ 1 bag (5 oz.) baby spinach
- ✦ 4 scallions, thinly sliced
- ✦ 1 pint grape tomatoes, halved

Serves: 4
Total Cook Time: 30-35 minutes
Temperature Setting: 350 degrees

DIRECTIONS:

1. Add olive oil to a casserole dish and bake for 5 minutes at 350 degrees in your Nuwave Oven®.

2. Whisk the eggs with salt and pepper, adding in the tomatoes, spinach, scallions and Feta gradually. Stir gently.

3. Remove from oven and pour beaten eggs into the dish. Bake till browned around the edges.

4. Bake till the knife comes out of the cake completely clean, for roughly 25-30 minutes.

Moroccan Pork Kebab

A pork dish with Moroccan flavors? Yes, it exists! These bite sized kebabs on wooden skewers are great for entertaining friends on a movie night. The charred flavor gives it that extra Moroccan punch.

INGREDIENTS:

+ 1 ½ pound pork loin, boneless, cut into 1 ½ inch pieces
+ 1 eggplant, cut into 1 inch pieces with skin
+ Pita bread to serve
+ 1 red onion, cut in 8 wedges
+ ½ pint Moroccan tzatziki sauce (cucumber yogurt sauce)
+ 1 tbsp. tomato paste
+ 1 tbsp. cumin, ground
+ 1 garlic clove, chopped
+ 1/8 tsp cinnamon, ground
+ 4 tbsp. olive oil
+ ¾ tsp black pepper
+ 1 ½ tsp kosher salt
+ 2 tbsp. chopped mint leaves
+ ½ cucumber, sliced
+ ¼ cup orange juice

Serves: 4
Total Cook Time: 45 minutes
Temperature Setting: 425 degrees

DIRECTIONS:

1. Preheat the Nuwave Oven® to 425 degrees.

2. Combine tomato paste, orange juice, cumin, cinnamon, garlic, 2 tbsp. oil, 1 tsp salt and 1 tsp pepper. Rub this dressing onto the pork pieces, cover and refrigerate for eight hours.

3. In a bowl, combine onion, oil, salt, and pepper with eggplant pieces. In the Nuwave , bake the onion and eggplant for 20 minutes.

4. Alternately place the pork, eggplant and onion pieces onto wooden skewers and place them onto a baking tray. Bake the skewers for 25 minutes.

5. During the last 5 minutes, place the break onto the skewers.

6. To serve, spoon the tzatziki on the slide of the serving plate containing kebab skewers, sprinkle with cucumber and mint.

Basil Pesto Meatballs with Couscous

One can never have enough exotic flavors! These versatile meatballs can actually be served with anything, yet is best served with couscous. Fresh basil pesto coats each mouth watering meatball for an Italian taste.

INGREDIENTS:

+ 1 ½ lbs. ground beef
+ ½ cup bread crumbs
+ ¾ cup basil pesto
+ 3 tbsp. olive oil
+ 1 egg
+ 10 oz. couscous
+ ¼ cup parmesan cheese, grated
+ Kosher salt, to taste
+ Black pepper, to taste

Serves: 4
Total Cook Time: 25 minutes
Temperature Setting: 350 degrees

DIRECTIONS:

1. Grease a baking tray with 2 tbsp. olive oil.

2. Place the beef in a bowl and add in bread crumbs, ½ cup pesto, salt, and pepper. Shape the mixture into meatballs with ¼ cup mixture for each.

3. Place the meatballs on the tray and bake in your Nuwave Oven® at 350 degrees for 15 minutes plus an additional 10 minutes, flipping the meatballs.

4. Combine ¼ cup basil pesto and 1 tbsp. olive oil to coat each meatball. Sprinkle with parmesan.

5. To serve, place cooked couscous and meatballs in each plate.

Chicken Flautas with Sour Cream

This is a Mexican's dream straight from your favorite authentic Mexican restaurant! These flautas are easy to prepare and looks great on the plate. Serve it with sour cream, guacamole, picante sauce or Spanish rice for a wholesome meal.

INGREDIENTS:

✦ 2 boneless chicken breasts, cut in half

✦ 8 oz. picante sauce

✦ ¼ tsp cumin, ground

✦ 8 oz. cheddar cheese, shredded

✦ 8 oz. Montery Jack cheese, shredded

✦ 36 corn tortillas

Serves: 36, great for crowds!
Total Cook Time: 15-25 minutes
Temperature Setting: 450 degrees

DIRECTIONS:

1. In a bowl, combine picante sauce, cumin, and shredded chicken.

2. Heat oil in a skillet over medium heat. Heat each corn tortilla for 1 to 2 seconds on either side until softened in your Nuwave Oven® at 450 degrees.

3. In the middle of each tortilla, put 1 tbsp. of the chicken mixture. Sprinkle the cheese mixture on top and roll the tortilla, placing them on a cookie sheet.

4. Seaming the sides, bake the tortillas in the oven for 15-25 minutes till crispy.

Sausages with Maple Sauce and Figs

Using maple sauce and figs with sausage might sound a little off putting. However, the sweetness of the two balances out the meaty saltiness of sausages really well. Make some on your own to find out!

INGREDIENTS:

- ✦ 2 tbsp. Balsamic vinegar
- ✦ 2 packets roasted garlic sausages
- ✦ 2 tbsp. Maple Syrup
- ✦ 8 figs, ripe
- ✦ 2 tbsp. olive oil
- ✦ 1 ½ lbs. Swiss chard
- ✦ ½ sweet onion, large
- ✦ Salt and pepper to season

Serves: 4
Total Cook Time: 20-22 minutes
Temperature Setting: 450 degrees

DIRECTIONS:

1. Mix 1 tbsp. vinegar and maple syrup in a small bowl. Place the sausages and figs on foil lined oven tray, brush with the mixture.

2. Roast for 8-10 minutes at 450 degrees in your Nuwave Oven® till heated through and golden, brushing the remaining syrup during half time.

3. Cook the onion in the Nuwave for 9 minutes; add in oil, ¼ tsp salt, ¼ tsp pepper, and the remaining vinegar and heat for about 3 minutes more.

4. Serve Swiss chard with the dish.

DO YOU WANT COOKBOOKS LIKE THIS FOR FREE?

Get hundreds of amazing popular recipes in a convenient cookbook each month absolutely free. No catch.

Yes! You read correctly. We are doing this to build loyal fans who enjoy our work and support us through reviews.

You are not obligated to do anything. But if you like our cookbooks, please consider leaving a review on Amazon for us!It only takes you a minute, but leaves a huge impact for us as it helps new readers discover us.

SIGN UP NOW
COOKINGWITHAFOODIE.COM